YOUR MAGICAL

Nine steps to inspire creative cooking
Kate Marshall

Dedications

To Readers

The lovely thing about learning is that no one can take it away from you

To Phil

Who made me put in the recipes!

To Stephen

My chief food taster, who always makes me smile

Thank you for being there every step of the way

Acknowledgements

I have to start by thanking my wonderful husband, Stephen. From listening to my ideas for the book in the early days, through making me lunch when we were in lockdown, while I was head-down writing, to keeping me calm when I spent a frustrating day trying to get a chapter just right, only to tear it up for lack of inspiration. You were as important to this book getting finished as I was. I really would not have been able to do this without you.

Tuning an idea into a book is as challenging as it sounds, so I especially want to thank the individuals that helped make this happen:

My late dad, for encouraging me to be my own person, and my mum, for making me a better cook.

All my friends in the UK and Australia: the book would have been lesser if not for your feedback.

Huge thanks go to Caroline Kyriazis for designing the original Your Magical Kitchen website in four short weeks!

Camilla Carson for giving me great advice on how to get a book published, and Peter Shaw for encouraging me to follow my passion.

My terrific virtual team at Upwork: Manda Waller, Felicity Hall, James Hunter, Richard Fussey and Jamie Jones.

I am forever indebted to Phil Turner, managing director at Meze Publishing, who took on a new author at the height of the pandemic. I shall never forget that day. All hail the awesome team at Meze, who worked tirelessly to get the book done. Special thanks go to editor Katie Fisher, creative director Paul Cocker, publishing manager Emma Toogood, PR and social media manager Lizzy Capps and to freelance food photographer Paul Gregory.

To my followers on Instagram, thank you for cheering me on throughout the last eighteen months. I love engaging with you and learning about your own cooking stories.

Last but not least, I want to thank everyone who has bought this book. I know how hard it is to learn to cook well. I would love cooking to come naturally to everyone, because I genuinely believe it is a zen thing: comforting, creative, convivial. No doubt I am bound to have made some errors in the book, here and there, for which I hope you can forgive me, but if you pick up even a few tips and techniques, I hope you find it worthwhile and joyful.

YOUR MAGICAL KITCHEN

First edition printed in 2021 in the UK

ISBN: 978-1-910863-83-1

Edited by: Katie Fisher & Phil Turner

Photography by: Paul Gregory

Design origination by:
Richard Fussey & James Hunter

Cover illustration by: Jamie Jones

Typography by: Paul Cocker

PR: Emma Toogood & Lizzy Capps

Contributors: Lucy Anderson,
Suki Broad, Katherine Dullforce,
Felicity Hall, Michael Johnson,
Lizzie Morton, Manda Waller

Printed and bound in the UK by
Bell & Bain Ltd, Glasgow

Published by Meze Publishing Limited
Unit 1b, 2 Kelham Square
Kelham Riverside
Sheffield S3 8SD
Web: www.mezepublishing.co.uk
Telephone: 0114 275 7709
Email: info@mezepublishing.co.uk

STARTERS

"Cooking is one of the most zen things – you have to be there." Roy Choi

Your Magical Kitchen was created for those of you who love to eat and are happy to cook yet find yourselves less confident about producing restaurant-quality food in your own kitchen. This isn't a recipe book per se, nor is it a book about cooking techniques like searing a steak or poaching an egg. There are plenty of videos on the internet to help you with that. It's not an introduction to cooking either. Your Magical Kitchen is a method for learning how to eat well every day, based on the foods you love to eat and the dishes you adore, with the aim of expanding your culinary horizons. It's about looking forward to getting into your kitchen, feeling comfortable in your space and no longer having to shy away from a place that has perhaps become a dumping ground for half-used packets of long-forgotten ingredients.

Eating is one thing. Cooking is another. What connects them is food: food is the fuel, recipes are the roadmap and cooking is the journey. You decide where you want to go, helped by a magical kitchen that inspires you. It doesn't need to be flash. It doesn't need to be that big. Nor does it need to be filled with every utensil and appliance under the sun. It just needs to stock the foods that you love to eat, brought together with foodstuffs that you need to make the dishes that you want to cook. Nothing is worse than flinging open your fridge, pantry, cupboards and drawers only to draw a blank. Essential ingredients missing. Foods past their use-by date. Too few foods that go together. Your Magical Kitchen provides the foundation for cooking the dishes you want to make. A place where imagination and invention run free. Somewhere that alchemy and metamorphosis take place. The culinary equivalent of a treasure trove into which you can dip at any time, for any meal.

A little about me

I love cooking. Never a week goes by without me finding some new idea for a dish or a meal. Inspiration comes from all sorts of places: magazine articles, restaurant reviews, a newly discovered deli, a holiday recounted, a fond memory jolted. Sometimes the idea spurs me into immediate action and off I go to the market: a woman on a mission. At other times, it just hangs around like a forlorn dog waiting for its mistress to take it out for a spin. I'm happy being a home cook and I don't feel the need to turn out spectacular dishes day-in, day-out. I buy the occasional takeaway when I'm tired from work, and I cheat my way through a frangipane tart using shop-bought pastry, all without ever feeling guilty.

I do not pretend to be a professional cook. I have my bad days in the kitchen, just like everyone else, but I don't let them get me down. Had I wanted culinary perfection at the outset, I would have taken a year off and gone to one of those catering colleges that cookery websites and magazines are always promoting. Perfection was not what I was after. Joy and happiness in the kitchen were always my goals.

I learnt to cook in my mum's kitchen. By today's standards she had a relatively small repertoire; traditional British (roasts), classical French (coq au vin) and conventional Italian (lasagne) alongside anglicised versions of Chinese and Indian recipes. These were her standbys. Sharing a love of all things sweet, we occasionally ventured into American cuisine, turning out cherry pies, brownies and angel cakes. Recipe books that introduced us to more exciting and exotic cuisines, however, were rare. Even when we came upon them, many of the necessary ingredients proved too hard to find, or too expensive to buy.

The first kitchen that I could call my own was nothing more than a two-hob burner, a mini fridge and a floor-to-wall pantry in a typical cramped Greenwich bedsit, rather like Rachel Khoo's 'Little Paris Kitchen'. I was in my last year at university and I assumed I'd stay there after finals, but unexpectedly my father was invited to take up a job in Australia. The three of us decamped to Canberra, where I worked for a couple of years before moving to Sydney. I fell in love with the Emerald City and even more with the food scene, which combined local produce with Mediterranean and Asian influences.

The only downside of the city's kinetic energy for me was the tension between whether to eat out or cook in. I was striding out in a time when self-declared feminists (which every woman – or at least every Western woman – was expected to be) felt they had far better things to do than chain themselves to the kitchen sink. All my girlfriends had read *The Handmaid's Tale*. We all shuddered. So we also cooked less as a result. Many of us 'chose' to throw off the shackles our stay-at-home mothers had lamented, quietly abandoned our pinnies and adopted shiny suits that came with sharper lines than the wings of a Boeing 747.

Behind closed doors, I kept cooking, building up my skills and learning how to make some of the trickier things that a 'good cook' had to conquer (shortcrust pastry, soufflés, béarnaise sauce and omelettes). I cooked for myself, but far less for others. I joined in with the fun of eating out, but between courses I sneaked away to quiz the maître d' or waiter about the ingredients and how they had been brought together. I jotted notes on napkins (this being a time before smartphones were commonplace) and filed them in my kitchen drawers for future use.

Fast-forward a few years on, while I was still cooking underground, and something shifted in the culture. British restaurant critic Nigella Lawson launched her first book, *How To Eat*, which enjoyed huge popularity. Home cooking came back into fashion. Her second book, *How to Be a Domestic Goddess*, was even more influential. We home cooks were no longer subjugated slaves but sensuous sirens, taking command of hearth and home. To this day, I don't know why this cultural shift happened, but we certainly did a 180-degree turn and went back into the kitchen. The result of all this was the rise of the Supercook.

Being a Supercook was hard work. Where previously two or three bottles of oil in the pantry had sufficed, a dozen now seemed to be too few. Every variety known to humankind found its way into my pantry, as did flavour-infused vinegars, dozens of herbs, spices and countless sauces and pastes. This ridiculous accumulation of foodstuffs (as opposed to fresh foods) didn't stop there. My own collection of pasta, noodles and rice made Imelda Marcos's shoe collection look meagre by comparison. Indulgence was firmly on the rise. My food budget increased sharply, while my waste bins bulged with foods that had passed their use-by dates, purchased in a bout of unfounded optimism. More worryingly, I had a sneaking suspicion that my ability to produce a well-thought-out meal was actually diminishing.

One summer evening, getting ready to cook while listening to Bruce Springsteen belting out *57 Channels (And Nothin' On)*, I knew the game was up. Like the number of cable TV channels popping up almost daily, my kitchen was stuffed to the gills, and yet held nothing to eat. I sank to the floor and started to cry (I know, I know, all very dramatic).

Time to change

When you love doing something that you feel is intrinsic to who you are, making changes is quite hard to do. I was in the doldrums for a good few days before I decided I needed some help. I turned to one of my friends, who ran a concierge service for professional dinkies who wanted to pay someone else to do the essential – but often boring – chores of running a home. This was years before we got into tidying up and decluttering our stuff, courtesy of Marie Kondo. My friend was a not only a clean freak, but also a brilliant cook. One sweep of her kitchen, pantry, baking cupboards, fridge and freezer taught me enough to break my cycle of over-stocking and opened my mind to the idea of shopping smartly. She also encouraged me to buy foods that would go together, rather than pick random stuff off the supermarket shelves willy-nilly.

I went back to my kitchen and cleaned out my freezer, fridge and all my cupboards. During this task, it occurred to me suddenly that no two cooks would have identical likes and dislikes when it came to food, which had to mean that no two kitchens would stock the same ingredients. Which foods and foodstuffs I stored in my kitchen would not be the same in any other cook's kitchen. So what was the purpose of following someone else's pantry/cupboard/fridge lists? Why wouldn't I just create my own lists, based on the foods that I liked to eat?

What I also learnt in the process of cleaning out my kitchen was that despite being able to cook a reasonable range of dishes, I wasn't exactly sure *why* they were good. Also, why wasn't I creating my own recipes based on the foods I liked to eat? Not that I knew it right there and then, but on reflection, I think that was when the idea of a magical kitchen was born. In that moment, I made a decision: from then on, I would think food first, recipes second.

Time to act

As my thinking and my cooking developed, I played around with different models and concepts for stocking the magical kitchen that I was after. What I landed on (very likely inspired by the TV show *Grand Designs*) was to separate out the foundations, fixtures and finishes of cooking, in the same way that you would build a house:

✦ **Foundations** would be foods that I liked to eat, based on taste and flavour.

✦ **Fixtures** would be foodstuffs like herbs, spices, condiments, wines, spirits and liqueurs that would add extra flavour to the dishes I wanted to make.

✦ **Finishes** would be adornments to prettify my dishes with colour and garnishes for both everyday and special occasions.

I had to learn some things in order to get where I wanted to go, and books about cooking (rather than cookery books) played a big part in that. Some strokes of luck also came into play. I returned to the UK, for work, by which time the ever-decreasing cost of travel allowed me to immerse myself in cuisines that I had previously had to learn from magazines and books. I was blessed with jobs that took me to cities all over the world, interspersed with exotic holidays. Yet again, I badgered waiters wherever I went (this time with a smartphone!). Other waypoints included cookery courses: I went to Paris for a week with one of my foodie friends, where I brushed up on my patisserie skills and learnt how to make macarons, and the Resident Husband (he who eats) kindly gave me a voucher for Rick Stein's school in Cornwall, where I got over my love/hate relationship with fish (slimy to handle, but yummy to eat).

What I love most about my magical kitchen is its ability to adapt. It has worked for me in different circumstances (cooking for one, cooking for friends, cooking for family) and different kitchens, both small and large. It has supported me through autumnal weekends, dark wintry nights, crisp spring days, and long summer evenings. I would never have expected to cook three times a day in the various lockdowns that we have all had to manage during the worst months of the pandemic. Finding a delivery slot aside, I think my kitchen did well, facing down the challenges and getting us through the worst of it.

Over to you

I guarantee that it is well within your ability to create your own magical kitchen, regardless of its size and shape, the number of people for whom you cook and your cooking ability. If that seems like an over-confident claim, don't judge me just yet. My confidence in your ability to create this comes from experience, the usual trials and tribulations when experimenting with something new, and continuous testing.

First steps, as you know, are notoriously tricky. So, let me offer some reassurance upfront. None of the suggestions that I make for you will break the bank. I won't ask you to splash your cash on installing pantries or exchanging old appliances for new ones. You won't need to trot down to your local kitchen shop, buying up lots of shiny new cookware or bakeware. Nor will you need to search out exotic ingredients with eye-watering price tags simply because they have become the flavour of the month. You may want to buy some things as you go along, but you don't have to.

What we *are* going to do together is go through your cupboards and drawers, your fridge and your freezer, your pantry if you have one, and any spaces that you have set aside for cookery books, magazines and recipe folders. In a kitchen filled with joy, everything within it needs to have room to breathe. Next, we're going to bring in your favourite foods, which you can turn into your favourite dishes by working through the nine steps that follow. In short, we are going to create a kitchen that really performs.

So, if you want to know how to create your own magical kitchen, expand your culinary horizons and learn how to bring foods together in mouth-watering recipes, whether ones you want to follow or ones you want to make yourself, let's get going! Lastly, remember this:

Learning is finding out what you already know.
Doing is demonstrating that you know it.
Teaching is reminding others that they know just as well as you.
You are all learners, doers, teachers.
From Illusions by Richard Bach

FOUNDATIONS

FOODS

Ask your friends what their favourite foods are. Chances are they might say things like plant-based snacks, avocado toast, smoothies and everything that comes in a bowl, alongside more traditional options, like tacos, stir-fries, spaghetti Bolognese, pizza, mac and cheese, lasagne, curries, cheesecake and ice cream. As appetising as these things are, they are not foods: they are dishes.

Whatever dish you want to make – whether savoury, sweet, spicy or sour – you have to start with the underlying foods. Take mac and cheese, for example. It's a simple, savoury dish, made from pasta, milk, cheese, flour, butter and garlic (optionally) all of which are 'real' foods. Complex dishes like stir-fries start the same way but go further by adding some foodstuffs – like herbs, spices, oils, vinegars, sauces, pastes and alcohol – that take them in one of several culinary directions: African, American, Asian, European or Australian.

Each dish has a style of cooking characterised by distinctive ingredients, techniques and dishes, often associated with traditions and customs. If you wanted to cook all the dishes I listed above over a single week, you would have to buy a shedload of foods and foodstuffs to make them, largely because they span so many cuisines. Unless you were incredibly rich, stocking your kitchen with all the ingredients required to make these dishes would simply not be an option.

The remedy for balancing what you want to eat and what you can afford is choosing the foods that you love most and pairing them with foodstuffs to create healthy, tasty, flavoursome dishes.

Getting to grips with foods
✦ Go-To Foods
✦ Magical Foods
✦ Food Groups and Families

Go-To Foods are the foods you like to eat. They will be edible as they are (i.e. raw) or made edible through cooking (i.e. steamed, stewed, pan-fried or roasted). These are the foods that you will bring together to make delicious dishes. For example, if I am tempted into buying a dozen market-fresh leeks one week, I need to be sure I have enough Go-To Foods that typically go with leeks (chicken, ham, cheese and cream). Otherwise, I will generate waste. The more Go-To Foods you like, the greater the variety of dishes you can cook.

Magical Foods are a subgroup of your Go-To Foods. These are your must-have, can't-live-without, absolute favourites. Your Magical Foods are the cornerstone of your kitchen. They are the foods that you will buy regularly. Creating a smaller basket of Magical Foods helps you make better choices when you shop. I know that one of my absolute favourite foods – feta – goes well with at least four of my Go-To Foods (onions, green beans, root vegetables and peppers) because I know which tastes and flavours pair well with feta. Once you know which pairings and combinations work for the foods that you love, you will find it easier to stock your kitchen for the purposes of cooking all those delicious dishes that you want to make.

Food Groups cover the big five: proteins, vegetables, fruits, grains and dairy. Example foods for these groups include white fish, root vegetables, citrus fruits, pastas and cheeses. Each of these foods has a unique ratio of nutrients, based on the ratio of protein, fat, carbs, minerals, water and fibre, which influences which foods go best together.

Each Food Group contains a range of **Food Families** (see examples overleaf). If you like peaches and plums, you are drawing on foods from the stone fruits family (others include nectarines, apricots, damsons and cherries). The shoots and stems family includes asparagus, fennel, celery and artichoke, while the wet cheeses family includes mascarpone, mozzarella, ricotta, feta and queso.

Understanding these families helps you adapt recipes and make substitutions. For example, if you had a recipe in mind for a peach frangipane tart but no peaches to cook with, you could swap them for another stone fruit like apricots. The same goes for substituting peas with beans (from the peas, beans and pods family) or replacing tuna with mackerel (from the oily fish family). The Food Families I use come from Christine Ingram's *The World Encyclopaedia of Cooking Ingredients*, an amazing book, and if you do not have a copy of it, I would encourage you to buy it.

Shortcuts
Food Families

Proteins

Meats

Air-dried ham
Prosciutto, serrano, Bayonne

Bacon & gammon
Pancetta, speck, pastrami

Cooked ham
York, Virginia, jambon de Paris

Game
Quail, pheasant, rabbit

Poultry
Chicken, turkey, duck, goose

Red meats
Beef, veal, lamb, pork

Sausage & salami
Cumberland, chorizo, coppa

Offal
Liver, kidney

Seafood

Bivalves
Mussel, oyster, scallop, clam

Canned fish
Anchovy, pilchard, sardine

Cephalopods
Squid, cuttlefish, octopus

Crustaceans
Crab, lobster, prawn

Gastropods
Abalone, whelk, winkle

Deep sea fish
Swordfish, shark, marlin

Flat fish
Halibut, plaice, sole, turbot

Freshwater fish
Trout, salmon

Oily fish
Tuna, mackerel, anchovy

Miscellaneous fish
Skate, monkfish, John Dory

Round & flat fish
Sea bass, bream, cod, haddock, halibut, mullet, sole, plaice

Nuts
Hazelnut, almond, coconut, pistachio, walnut, pine, Brazil, macadamia

Seeds
Chia, linseed, sesame, poppy, sunflower, pumpkin

Vegetables & fruits

Vegetables

Alliums
Onion, shallot, garlic, leek, spring onion

Beans
Haricot, kidney, borlotti, cannellini, fava, black

Chinese greens
Pak choi, Chinese leaf, mustard green, choi sum

Green vegetables
Spinach, chard, cauliflower, broccoli, cabbage, kale, kohlrabi

Lentils & peas
Green, brown, red/yellow/green split, Puy

Mushrooms & fungi
White, oyster, shiitake, cep, morel, truffle, shimeji, straw

Peas, beans & pods
Pea, sweetcorn, okra, runner bean, green bean, soya, peanut

Plant-based
Tofu, bean curd, tempeh

Root vegetables
Potato, sweet potato, yam, celeriac, Jerusalem artichoke, parsnip, turnip, swede, carrot, beetroot

Salad vegetables
Watercress, mustard, cress, lettuce, rocket, chicory, radicchio, endive, cucumber, radish

Shoots & stems
Asparagus, fennel, celery, artichoke, Asian shoots

Sprouted beans
Alfalfa, mung, chickpea

Squashes
Courgette, pumpkin, butternut, marrow, gourd

Vegetable fruits
Tomato, pepper, chilli, aubergine, olive, avocado

Shortcuts
Food Families

Fruits

Apples & pears
Apple, pear, quince, medlar

Berries
Strawberry, raspberry, blueberry, blackberry, cranberry

Citrus fruits
Orange, lemon, lime, grapefruit, pomelo, kumquat, yuzu

Exotic fruits
Banana, date, kiwifruit, papaya, pineapple, pomegranate, dragon fruit

Other fruits
Melon, grape, fig, rhubarb

Stone fruits
Peach, mango, nectarine, apricot, plum, damson, cherry

Grains

Asian wrappers
Chinese pancake, spring roll wrapper, wonton skin, rice paper

Cereal grains
Bulgur, bran, couscous, semolina, polenta, popcorn, buckwheat, spelt, barley, oat, rye, quinoa

Flours
White, brown, cornflour, arrowroot

Noodles
Wheat, egg, rice, cellophane, soba

Pastas
Long, short, flat, stuffed

Rices
White, brown, basmati, risotto, Thai jasmine, short grain, long grain, glutinous, pudding, sushi, wild

Dairy

Milks

Dairy-based milks
Whole, skimmed, buttermilk, goat's, evaporated, condensed

Plant-based milks
Oat milk, almond milk, coconut milk, rice milk, soy milk

Cheeses

Blue cheeses
Stilton, Roquefort, Gorgonzola, Cambozola, Gippsland Blue

Hard cheeses
Cheddar, Comté, Gruyère, Parmesan, Manchego, Gouda

Natural rind cheeses
Crottin, Sancerre, Rocamadour

Semi-soft cheeses
Raclette, Reblochon, Taleggio, Edam, Havarti, Fresh Jack

Soft white cheeses
Brie, Camembert, Brillat-Savarin

Washed rind cheeses
Epoisses, Munster, Stinking Bishop

Wet cheeses
Fromage frais, mascarpone, mozzarella, ricotta, feta, queso

Butters
Salted/unsalted, margarine

Creams
Single/double, sour, crème fraiche, clotted

Fats
Lard, suet, shortening

Yoghurts
Natural, Greek, goat's, soya

Other

Eggs
Hen, quail, duck, goose

Coffees
Roast, espresso, Turkish

Chocolate
Dark, milk, white

Sweeteners
Demerara, brown, white sugar
Molasses, treacle, golden and maple syrup.
Honey – acacia, lavender, orange blossom, manuka

Teas
Black – Ceylon, Assam, Darjeeling
Green – gunpowder, matcha

Now that you have a feel for the different types of foods available to you, let's get going by **choosing your Go-To and Magical Foods.** When we get into the Taste and Flavour steps, you will see how Food Families help us pair, bounce and combine foods based on their unique properties.

To note, if you do most of the cooking in your household, choose the foods that you like to eat (as the French say, the family eats what the chef cooks!). If you are half of a team and share cooking responsibilities, base your foods on those that you both like to eat. Ready, then? Go back to the Food Families on pages 16 and 17 and choose the foods that you love and like. Here are a few tips to get you going:

✦ Clear your mind of dishes that you have cooked in the past. Focus on your favourite foods. Take as much time as you like and trust your gut. You already know what you like to eat.

✦ Using a pencil or pen, cross out the foods that you *don't* like to eat.

✦ Use a highlighter pen to identify 25 foods that are your absolute favourites: your Magical Foods. If you like, use the numbered lines opposite to write down the foods you've chosen.

What you have now is a **personalised list** of the foods you like and love to eat. Your Magical Foods will be the foundation of your kitchen, which your Go-To Foods will revolve around. Why 25 foods? Why not 10, 50 or 100? Well, almost half of us choose to do a big weekly shop. Allowing for takeaways, food-to-go and eateries, you'll likely get through most of your Magical Foods, assuming you'll include at least one and more likely two of those foods. Since these are the foods we love most, none of us would want to go without at least one of them in the dishes we make regularly! If you are making more than 10 meals a week, however, feel free to add a few more Magical Foods to your list.

Do this
Magical Foods

1. _____
2. _____
3. _____
4. _____
5. _____
6. _____
7. _____
8. _____
9. _____
10. _____
11. _____
12. _____
13. _____
14. _____
15. _____
16. _____
17. _____
18. _____
19. _____
20. _____
21. _____
22. _____
23. _____
24. _____
25. _____

Now you know which foods you like and love to eat, you need to remember them! I suggest you scan pages 16 and 17, which you worked on earlier, print it off and stick it on the inside of your pantry or one of your cupboards. I suggest this because we need to build on your Magical Foods list to identify the taste and flavour pairings that will go best with them, and so it's easier (and faster!) for you to pinpoint the foods and foodstuffs that you need to have in your kitchen.

Before we get into what you have found by making your list, it is worth noting that the more in-tune we are with our bodies, the more our bodies will ask us for certain types of food. With such a focus on wellbeing in our lives, we're starting to understand more and more about what kind of foods make us feel good, and which make us feel pretty crappy for a couple of days after eating them (giant pizzas with garlic bread and chips are often a strong contender here!).

For the growing number of vegetarians and vegans, there are enough substitutes now available that you can replace animal products in any dish. So, if you want to add a plant-based option to your list on the left, go right ahead!

Don't worry if there are whole Food Families (or Groups) that you don't care for, but do make a note of what that might mean for your diet if it's missing proteins, fats, vegetables, fruits or grains. Don't worry about the types of food you like or don't like either; for every Go-To or Magical Food, there will be any number of directions in which to take them: African, Asian, Caribbean, Chinese, European, Indian, Japanese, Korean, Mexican, Middle Eastern, Nordic, Persian, Peruvian. If chicken is on your list, for example, you can choose from West African chicken stew, Indian chicken samosas, Thai chicken thighs, French coq au vin, Caribbean jerk chicken, Japanese teriyaki chicken or Italian chicken parmigiana, to name just a few.

Despite good intentions, no chef, food writer, blogger or vlogger can tell you which foods you should like to eat. That said, you will probably be cooking for people who have different likes and dislikes to your own. For them, you can tweak your chosen dishes to accommodate their favourite foods, using the Food Families info as a guide.

Kate's List
Magical Foods

1. Almonds
2. Avocado
3. Beetroot
4. Cheese (Blue)
5. Cheese (Wet)
6. Chicken
7. Chocolate
8. Chorizo
9. Couscous
10. Cream/Milk
11. Garlic
12. Lamb
13. Lemons
14. Limes
15. Mushrooms
16. Oranges
17. Peaches
18. Pistachios
19. Prawns
20. Prosciutto
21. Raspberries
22. Strawberries
23. Sweetcorn
24. Tuna
25. Walnuts

I'm sharing my list of Magical Foods with you here, so that you can see how what you like to eat determines the dishes you want to cook. My list is choc-a-bloc with protein, dairy and fruit. There are four vegetables included (yet not one of them green) and only one grain (couscous). This means I have to dig deep into my second tier of Go-To Foods in order to achieve a more balanced diet. It is a constant challenge for me.

My list of Magical Foods should also give you some clues about which types of cuisines I prefer based on the foods I love. These nudge me into dishes that align naturally with Italian, Spanish and French cuisines. Asian cuisines get a nod – with a slight preference for Japanese over Chinese, and Indian over Vietnamese – and give me an entrée into Pacific Rim and Australasian cuisines. I struggle with Nordic dishes and while I enjoy Turkish, Middle Eastern and North African dishes when eating out, I don't cook these cuisines routinely because I am less proficient in them. Once you have gone through your Magical Foods list, you will see clues as to the type of dishes and cuisines that align with your food preferences.

Being mindful of the types of dishes and cuisines your favourite foods will serve best is an important element of your magical kitchen. The biggest payoff I got when I listed my Go-To Foods and Magical Foods was learning about which foods I needed in my kitchen that I could then pair and combine. It was also fantastic for me to learn how to expand the number of dishes I could cook, and how to adapt recipes by replacing my least-liked foods with foods that I could eat.

My journey with foods

How many of you remember the foods you least liked as a child? Foods that filled you with horror? I had a particularly tricky childhood in that respect. I refused to eat anything that came with a pit, pod, seed or bone (peppers, squashes, fish) and I gave a wide berth to foods that might pop or burst in my mouth (peas, tomatoes, kidney beans).

My apathy for large swathes of savoury foods that were prominent in many a household meal at that time was largely due to British cuisine, which Otto English described in his book, *Fake History,* was "nothing less than a ... crime scene". As a result, mum and I entered into a cooking pact. She was Main Course. I was Dessert.

On weekends, she would flip through her stash of Cordon Bleu magazines and pull out all the pots and pans required for some continental classic (beef bourguignon, Wiener schnitzel) while I hunted for the necessary ingredients in her well-stocked baking cupboard to whip up a Julia Child-inspired dessert. Charlotte Russe was a particular favourite; I was, and still am, a big fan of ladyfingers!

To give my mum her due, she never pushed me into eating foods that I disliked. No such benevolence during my boarding school years, however. Strict mistresses and starchy matrons gave short shrift to so much culinary pickiness. It took me years to work out what the problem was: an irrational fear of choking to death mid-meal. The medical term for this is pseudo dysphagia. People with this condition often have difficulty eating certain foods, which may have explained why I cooked milky puddings, soft trifles and smooth panna cottas. There is no family lore as to what might have sparked this; it's a mystery. Even now, I am far from a poster child for the balanced diet brigade...

My **Stardust Tip** for choosing your foods is to be open-minded. If you've never cooked a recipe or created a dish of your own for a favourite food, keep that food on your list. Often I hear friends say they don't know how to prepare a dish that they really enjoy – like steamed mussels with cream, garlic and parsley – which means they don't put mussels on their shopping list. Or they worry about buying a 'naughty 'food' stuffed with saturated fats. The first can be dealt with rationally (just have a go!) while the second is one for your conscience, but I do believe some naughtiness is too much fun to choose only once!

Next up are a few recipes that celebrate the wonder of fresh foods. Enjoy!

POSH BEET & FETA SALAD

I could eat beetroot and feta every day, but you can get into a rut when things stay the same. This is a pretty and delicious salad elevated by the marinated feta, which is a little more expensive but well worth it for the great flavour and texture.

Preparation time: 10 minutes | Cooking time: 25 minutes | Serves 2

INGREDIENTS

300g fresh red beetroot

100g fresh golden beetroot

50g whole almonds

75g watercress

200g marinated feta

For the dressing

60ml extra virgin olive oil

2 tbsp verjuice (I use the Maggie Beer brand)

1 tbsp maple syrup

Salt and pepper

METHOD

1. Remove the leaves from the beets, leaving some stalks. Boil the red beets in a large saucepan of water for 25 minutes, or until tender. In a separate pan, boil the golden beets for 15 minutes, or until tender.

2. While the beets are cooking, toast the almonds in a dry frying pan on a medium heat. They should be slightly charred. Leave to cool before roughly chopping.

3. Drain and refresh the cooked beets under cold running water, then peel and quarter them (the smaller golden beets may only need to be halved).

4. For the dressing, whisk all the ingredients together in a bowl and season with salt and pepper to taste.

5. Lay the beets and watercress on the serving plates, add the marinated feta, drizzle everything with the dressing and scatter with the chopped almonds.

NOTES

You can marinate your feta by putting the cheese into a clean jar and filling it with thyme, garlic salt, pepper, chilli flakes and good quality olive oil. Leave it to marinate overnight before using. Wear washing up gloves while handling the beetroot (before and after cooking) to avoid staining your hands. You can swap out the toasted almonds for pecans if you wish.

TUNA CEVICHE

This is so simple it almost doesn't need a recipe, but it's a good reminder to focus on the foods you like to eat and my mantra for creative cooking: foods first, recipes second. Tuna, limes and avocados are among my favourites and they come together wonderfully in this dish.

Preparation time: 10 minutes, plus 15 minutes marinating | Serves 2

INGREDIENTS

400g very fresh tuna

2 limes, juiced

1 tsp sea salt

6 French radishes

$\frac{1}{2}$ small fresh pineapple

$\frac{1}{2}$ fresh mango

$\frac{1}{2}$ cucumber, peeled and deseeded

Large bunch of fresh coriander

1 tbsp chilli flakes

2 avocados

1 tbsp olive oil

2 tbsp pomegranate molasses

1 packet of tortilla chips (I use Doritos Hint of Lime)

METHOD

1. Dice the tuna with a sharp knife into 2cm squares. Transfer the tuna to a glass bowl and add the lime juice and sea salt. Toss gently. Set aside for 15 to 20 minutes to marinate.

2. In the meantime, dice the radishes, pineapple, mango and cucumber into 2cm cubes. Tear the coriander into another glass bowl and add the chilli flakes along with the diced ingredients.

3. When you are almost ready to serve the ceviche, drain the marinated tuna and add it to the second bowl. Give the mixture a stir with a spoon.

4. Halve the avocados, remove the stone, scoop out the flesh and dice it into 2cm cubes. Gently fold the cubed avocado and olive oil into the tuna mixture.

5. Spoon the ceviche into your preferred serving bowl, then drizzle with the pomegranate molasses and serve with the tortilla chips on the side.

NOTES

You need to make this ceviche in a non-reactive bowl like glass, but once the ingredients are cured, you can serve the dish in a china or ceramic bowl if preferred. I use shop-bought tortilla chips to serve with this, but you can use tortilla wraps, cut into wedges and baked or fried.

LINGUINE ALLE ACCIUGHE

This is a deeply umami yet simple pasta dish with anchovies. Leftover crusty bread is perfect for this, but even 3-day-old white or brown bread will do. Don't skimp on the garlic though, you do need it all and the dish will be weaker if you use less.

Preparation time: 10 minutes | Cooking time: 10-15 minutes | Serves 2

INGREDIENTS

200g linguine

100g slightly stale bread

5 cloves of garlic

1 tsp lemon zest

1 tsp table salt

$\frac{1}{2}$ tsp ground pepper

30ml olive oil

3 anchovy fillets in oil

2 tsp lemon juice

30g parmesan (or Pecorino, for a saltier taste)

15g thyme, finely chopped

1 tbsp unsalted butter

METHOD

1. Put a large pan of salted water on a medium heat for the pasta. Cut the hard crusts off the bread and blitz the rest in a food processor to make crumbs. Chop 4 of the garlic cloves and add them to the processor with the lemon zest. Blitz again, then add the salt and pepper.

2. Heat 10ml of the olive oil in a frying pan over a medium heat. Fry the garlicy breadcrumbs in the oil, stirring often, for about 5 minutes until golden brown and crisp. Use a slotted spoon to transfer them to a small bowl.

3. Add the remaining olive oil to the same pan over a low-medium heat. Add the anchovies and cook for 1 minute (or more) until dissolved. Slice the remaining garlic clove and fry it with the anchovies until crisp, then stir in the lemon juice.

4. Bring the pan of salted water to the boil, then add the linguine and cook for about 3 minutes, stirring occasionally, until al dente.

5. Drain the linguine carefully over the sink, reserving around 30ml of the pasta water. Put the pan back on the hob over a medium heat and add the parmesan. Toss with the linguine until melted, then add the anchovy-garlic mix and stir gently so that it coats the pasta.

6. Remove the pan from the heat and add the thyme, butter and half of the crispy breadcrumbs. Toss until combined and the butter has melted. If the pasta seems dry, add some of the cooking water and toss again. Season with salt and pepper to taste and stir in a little more lemon juice if desired.

7. Divide the pasta between bowls using two forks. Top with the remaining breadcrumbs to serve.

NOTES

You can add chilli (fresh or dried) if you like, but I like to sink into the savouriness of this dish without the spice.

NORWEGIAN CREAM PUDDING

There are a few desserts that I can make from memory and this is one of them. Who can resist a jammy-custard dessert, crowned with Cadbury chocolate flakes? I have made this dish more times than I can remember and always love it.

Preparation time: 15 minutes | Cooking time: 15-20 minutes | Serves 4

INGREDIENTS

450g apricot, peach or cherry jam
5 very large eggs
25g white caster sugar
1 tsp vanilla essence
600ml whole milk
80ml double cream
2 Cadbury Flakes

METHOD

1. Preheat the oven to 170°c. Fill a deep roasting tin half-full of water and put it in the oven. Spread the jam over the base of a large, ovenproof soufflé dish (mine is 20cm in diameter).

2. Break 4 of the eggs into a large bowl and separate the last egg. Add the extra egg yolk to the bowl along with the sugar and vanilla essence. Whisk until the mixture is pale cream in colour.

3. Heat the milk in a saucepan to a low boil, then pour it into the bowl with the eggs, sugar and vanilla. Whisk to combine the liquids thoroughly.

4. Strain the mixture through a fine sieve into the soufflé dish so it covers the layer of jam. Cover the dish with greaseproof paper, then carefully place it into the roasting tin, making sure the water doesn't splash into the pudding or come over the sides.

5. Cook the pudding in the preheated oven for 40 to 45 minutes until firm to the touch. Give the dish a gentle shake to make sure it has set.

6. Leave the pudding to cool at room temperature for at least 30 minutes and preferably a couple of hours.

7. When the pudding is ready to serve, whip the double cream to soft peaks. Use an electric whisk to whip the remaining egg white to stiff peaks, then fold the egg white into the cream.

8. Spoon the cream onto the pudding and smooth out to form an even layer, then swirl into small peaks. Break the flakes into 4 pieces and drop them on top. Serve in individual bowls.

NOTES

If you have any pudding leftover or there are only 2 to 3 people eating, keep the rest in the fridge for the next day. There are several versions of this dish online, though mine is lighter as it uses whole milk for the custard rather than double cream.

TASTES

Taste is the bedrock for cooking a great dish. We use the words taste and flavour interchangeably but in truth, they are different things. Taste and flavour are two sides of a coin and that coin is food. Taste refers specifically to the five basic tastes that we perceive in our mouth, like salty and sour. Flavour refers specifically to a vast range of aromas, like earthy or fruity, that we perceive through our nose. Cheffy-chefs are well versed in the differences between taste and flavour, and that's what often gives them the edge over us home cooks.

Despite the fact that we all breathe the same air, take in rays from the same sun, and hydrate our bodies with water and other liquids, we don't have the exact same experiences when it comes to taste. For example, some people who have more bumps on their tongue (papilla) usually find some tastes too spicy or fiery, while certain people need six spoonfuls of sugar in their coffee or tea to get the same level of satisfaction and reward that others get with only two.

Almost everyone can recognise the five classic tastes (bitter, salty, sour, sweet and umami) but the different chemicals that we have can make the range of those tastes differ. This means we will all have different reactions to the same food. That said, people don't generally confuse sweet tastes with sour ones, or bitter tastes with salty ones, so you can follow the principles of taste pairing regardless of how many bumps you have!

Creating tasty dishes is a fundamental skill and, like all skills, you learn through practice. What drives us to acquire these skills depends on our motivations. Do you eat to live, or live to eat? Are you simply happy messing around in your kitchen? Or are you interested in learning about other cuisines and expanding your culinary horizons? Whatever your motive, understanding what makes food tasty begins here.

Getting to grips with tastes

✦ Taste Families

✦ Texture Families

✦ Taste and Texture Pairings

To the five classic **Taste Families** recognised in cooking, I have added another three. If in doubt about which food belongs to which Taste Family, try conjuring up words that are similar to those used most often when describing tastes. Often, you will see these in recipes where chefs and cooks use synonyms to avoid repeating themselves, such as the following:

✦ Bitter – cutting, acerbic, tart

✦ Salty – marine, briny, brackish

✦ Umami – savoury, yeasty, bone-warming, hearty, malty

✦ Sour – lip-puckering, tart, acidic, citrusy, vinegary, tangy

✦ Sweet – dulcet, saccharine, honeyed, fresh, ripe, sugary

✦ Fatty – oily, greasy, lardy

✦ Spicy – hot, fiery, peppery, piquant, racy

✦ Astringent – biting, harsh, sharp

You don't need to create a list of your favourite tastes, but what I recommend you do next is identify the taste of each of your Magical Foods using the Taste Family Wheel, (see page 35). If you can't find a match, just do a quick internet search. If you like, you can knock-up a simple list of your own – something like the below – and stick it next to your Go-To and Magical Foods list.

Food	Food Group	Food Family	Taste
Lemon	Fruit	Citrus Fruits	Sour
Tuna	Protein	Oily Fish	Salty

This will help you in two ways: understanding which tastes you like, and what that means for the type of dishes and cuisines you like, such as spicy beef stir-fries or umami chicken katsu. You will also discover **contrasting** but complementary tastes that bring out the best in each other (like salty ham and sweet-sour pineapple) and **balancing** tastes that create harmony (like bananas and chocolate). For further notes on examples of pairings, see page 40, and examples of how to pair tastes on pages 42-43.

Regardless of where foods come from or where they end up, the Taste Families to which they belong are universally recognised. Indian ghee, for example, belongs to the fatty family not because it is an Indian food, but because of its chemical structure (in this case, based on fatty acids). Other foods that belong to this family include butter and animal fats in northern and temperate countries.

As you can see from these examples, Mother Nature created tasty foods for every climate, hot or cold, wet or dry. Before foods like these could travel across the world, local cuisines were reliant on a much smaller range of ingredients. That meant the dishes they made would track with the fruits, vegetables, dairy products, nuts and grains that were locally available, yet part of a bigger picture in which similar tastes flourished. For home cooks, this approach is an absolute blessing, as you will see when we get into Taste Pairings.

Shortcuts
Taste Families

Foods

Descriptors

Taste

Most meats (red in particular), including sausages, salamis, hams and bacon, most types of fish and cheese, eggs and some nuts (peanuts).

Tomatoes, mushrooms, parmesan, seaweed, anchovies, yeast, soy sauce.

Brassicas (cabbage, Brussels sprouts, kale, cauliflower, broccoli), salad vegetables (chicory, endive, rocket, mustard), ginger, olives, some nuts (walnuts), coffee and cocoa.

Butter, ghee, oils, animal fats, some nuts (coconut), avocado.

Savoury, yeasty, bone-warming, hearty, malty

Marine, briny, brackish

Cutting, acerbic, tart

Creamy, lardy, oily

Umami

Salty

Fat

Bitter

Cranberries, pomegranates, green bananas and apples

Biting, harsh, sharp

Sweet

Astringent

Sour

Spicy

Dulcet, saccharine, honeyed, fresh, ripe, sugary, zippy

Lip-puckering, tart, acidic, citrusy, vinegary, tangy

Hot, fiery, peppery, piquant, racy

Milk, grains (wheat, rice, barley), creamy fruits (bananas, mangoes, stone fruits), earthy root vegetables (carrots, potatoes, beetroots), some nuts (almonds, hazelnuts, pecans).

Cirtus fruits (limes, lemons, grapefruits), cherries, rhubarb, currants, tamarind, buttermilk, sour cream, yoghurts, fermented vegetables.

Chillies, capsicums, Szechuan peppercorns.

Texture Families are the second thing you need to wrap your head around to make tasty dishes.

There is a finite number of words used to describe the texture of foods. If you describe a food as 'crispy' (such as roast potatoes or bacon) then I am likely to describe that food in the same way. Having not come across a comprehensive book on the textures of foods, I chose to make up my own Texture Families, drawing largely on descriptors in cookery books and magazine recipes. The two things I took away from that small project were these.

First, recognising that there are no better or worse textures (i.e. each texture has value in its own right). Second, what matters for the dishes that you want to make is choosing foods with a range of textures that are different from, and ideally the opposite of, the main ingredient. You do not want an entrée built on a fresh, crunchy cos lettuce to include crunchy, toasted nuts. What you need with the cos is a creamy yet sour lemony yoghurt dressing. Too many similar textures in one dish can turn off your taste buds. In short, texture pairings are mostly about contrast and rarely about harmony.

Shortcuts
Texture Families

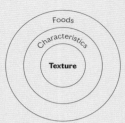

Foods

Characteristics

Texture

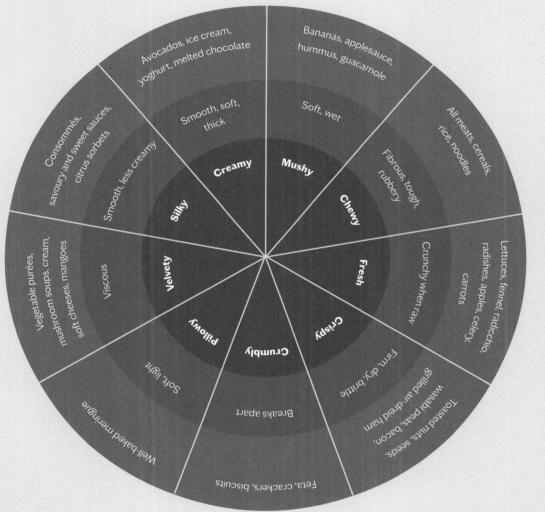

Avocados, ice cream, yoghurt, melted chocolate

Bananas, applesauce, hummus, guacamole

Consommés, savoury and sweet sauces, citrus sorbets

Smooth, soft, thick

Soft, wet

All meats, cereals, rice, noodles

Smooth, less creamy

Creamy

Mushy

Fibrous, tough, rubbery

Vegetable purées, mushroom soups, cream, soft cheeses, mangoes

Silky

Chewy

Lettuces, fennel, radicchio, radishes, apples, celery, carrots

Viscous

Velvety

Fresh

Crunchy when raw

Pillowy

Crispy

Crumbly

Firm, dry, brittle

Toasted nuts, seeds, wasabi peas, bacon, grilled air-dried ham

Soft, light

Breaks apart

Well-baked meringue

Feta, crackers, biscuits

The best dishes bring different foods together through **Taste and Texture Pairings**. Some dishes revolve around a single dominant ingredient. Other dishes will be more of a mix of ingredients, evenly distributed, like an Asian slaw for example. Some dishes only need two foods to make an impact: imagine fresh prawns piled on creamy avocado, or sour cream with spicy peppers. Our traditional English breakfast is a celebration of textures; part of what makes this dish great is the combination of crispy bacon, juicy sausages, crunchy fried bread, runny eggs, sloppy baked beans and soft tomatoes. At the other end of the spectrum is a trifle with all its soft components: liqueur-soaked sponge and wobbly jelly, onto which you pile velvety custard, topped with silky Chantilly cream and a mountain of fresh strawberries.

I follow the principles of taste pairing from James Briscione's book, *The Flavor Matrix*, because he set it out so simply. While he focused on flavours (and how to pair them), he kindly threw in a 'How to Pair Tastes' diagram too, setting out all of the different complementary and balancing tastes. Complementary tastes are pairings that bring out the best in one another, such as sweet and salty foods (think salted caramel). Balancing tastes are pairings that oppose one another to create harmony, such as sour foods playing down sweet ones (think raspberry pavlovas).

You can see complementary taste pairings in classic dishes, such as:

- ✦ **Salty** foods with **sweet** foods (prosciutto and melon, ham and pineapple)
- ✦ **Sour** foods with **spicy** foods (lemon and chillies, sour cream and jalapeños)
- ✦ **Umami** foods with **salty** foods (beef and tomatoes, mushrooms and eggs)

And balancing taste pairings, such as:

- ✦ **Sweet** foods with **bitter** foods (bananas and chocolate, almonds and coffee)
- ✦ **Umami** foods with **bitter** foods (tomatoes and rocket, bacon and brussels sprouts)
- ✦ **Fatty** foods with **sour** foods (avocados and lime, butter and lemon)

If you can take an hour or so, look through your current recipes to find the ones that align with the principles of pairing above. Remember, we're *not yet* including the flavours of your favourite foods, so focus on the tastes included in those recipes.

Now we'll look at texture pairings. These are some classic examples:

✦ Croutons (crispy, heavy) atop a caramelised French onion soup (silky, heavy)

✦ Iceberg lettuce (crisp, light) with a yoghurt dressing (velvety, heavy)

✦ Butter lettuce (fresh, light) with an oil and lemon dressing (silky, heavy)

✦ Grilled tortillas (crispy, heavy) with melting cheese (creamy, heavy)

✦ Cold veal (chewy, heavy) with a rich sauce made from tuna, mayonnaise and capers (silky, heavy)

✦ Battered cod (chewy, heavy) served with chips (crispy, heavy) and peas (mushy, heavy)

✦ Cooked prawns (chewy, heavy) and avocados (creamy, heavy) with radicchio (fresh, light)

✦ Amaretti biscuits (crumbly, light) sprinkled over baked apricots (creamy, heavy)

✦ Meringue shells (pillowy, light) served with a cherry sauce (velvety, heavy)

Did you spot the pairings where the texture of the foods was the same, but required a different add-on due to the weight of them? Ten points if you chose the two lettuces in the list. Both are fresh foods, but the iceberg is more robust, enabling it to carry a heavier and thicker dressing.

Taste and texture pairings come easily to cooks because we all acquire taste memory over time, and because there are well-understood pairing principles to guide you. Most seasoned cooks know that a squeeze of lemon juice (sour) will cut through a too-buttery sauce (fatty), or that most cheeses (salty or sour) eat well with a relish (sweet or spicy) at the end of a meal.

Shortcuts
Taste Pairings
Complementary

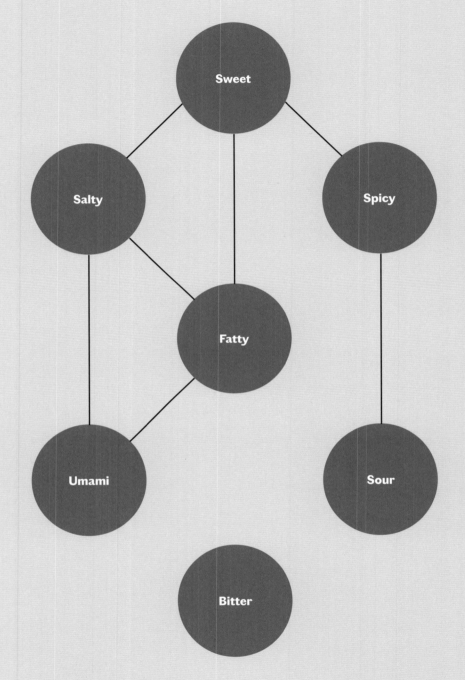

The Flavor Matrix,
James Briscione

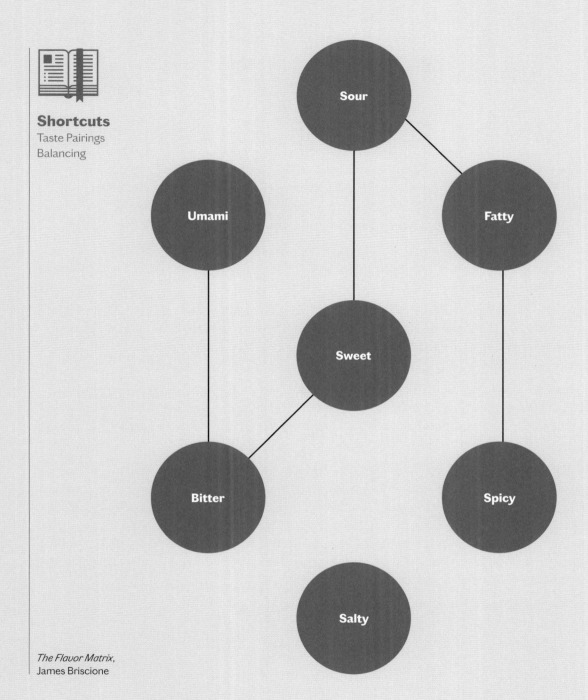

Sour

Umami

Fatty

Sweet

Bitter

Spicy

Salty

The Flavor Matrix,
James Briscione

My journey with tastes

Anyone who has moved from a northern climate to a southern one knows what a difference a few degrees of latitude can make. I arrived in Australia at the same time modern Australian cuisine – aka Mod Oz – was emerging, offering Mediterranean dishes with Asian and Middle Eastern influences. It was a long, long way from the stodge that made up most British food and the heaviness of French haute cuisine that I had been used to.

Foods I had never seen before included: kiwi fruits; mangoes; papayas; pomegranates; semi-soft Italian cheeses; calamari; John Dory; pak choi; Chinese leaf; mustard greens; Balmain bugs; and king, tiger, banana and endeavour prawns. From a culinary perspective, this was a game-changer for me.

Foods which I had previously skirted around as a child but now felt brave enough to try included all those bony fishes, seedy peppers and chillies, stone and pod fruits and vegetables. These were a revelation on their own, but even more revelatory to me was the lushness of the food, the lightness of the dishes and the 'flavour bombs' that chefs created, using the five classic tastes all at once.

It's so much easier to learn about taste and texture pairings in situ, because you can bombard everyone around you, asking questions, taking pictures and making a note or two, which you can refer to once you're back at home. That said, there are, of course, plenty of cook books and websites containing millions of recipes from which you can draw inspiration.

My **Stardust Tip** for tempting your taste buds is to follow the principles of taste and texture pairings, and adjust for your palate. Keep an eye on the ratio of ingredients set out in recipes that you have found, or created on your own. For example, I love spicy dishes, but only up to a point. I am not good with red-hot fiery chillies, so I often swap them out for mustard seeds to reduce the heat of the dish, or add cooler liquids like coconut milk. Happily, textures are far more forgiving and more tangible. Rarely do I hear someone say they dislike velvety dishes, like a roasted garlic soup. Nor do I often hear anyone celebrating mushy foods. If you're not that keen on introducing too many tastes in a single dish, at least offset those tastes with some interesting textures!

More recipes now for creating really yummy, tasty dishes.

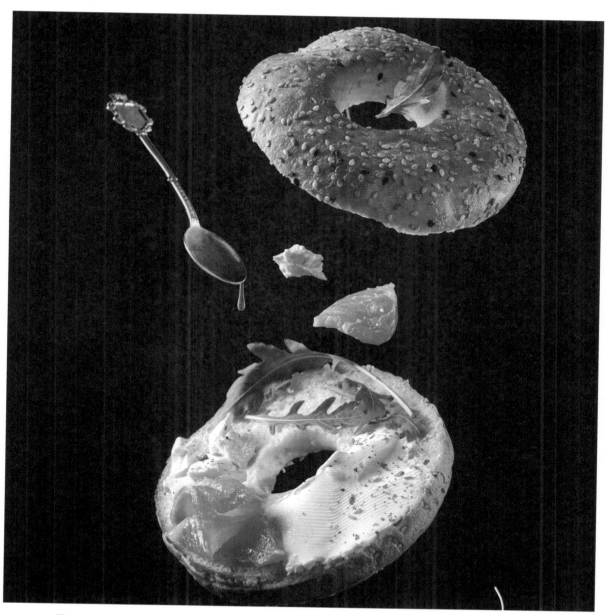

Taste as you go. When you taste the food throughout the cooking process
you can make adjustments as you go.
Anne Burrell

SPANISH SERRANO HAM, SPINACH & AVOCADO SALAD

The warm dressing really makes this salad stand out: the hit of sherry vinegar with softened red onions and savoury stock tastes amazing. The avocados add brightness and velvetiness. I have made this dish forever and it's never failed me. A simple but stunning combination of tastes and textures.

Preparation time: 10 minutes | Cooking time: 10 minutes | Serves 2

INGREDIENTS

200g baby leaf spinach
90g Spanish serrano ham
1 tbsp olive oil
2 large red onions
2 tbsp sherry vinegar
1 Oxo beef stock cube
100ml warm water
2 avocados

METHOD

1. Wash the baby leaf spinach and transfer to a large serving bowl. Place the strips of serrano ham under a hot grill until crisp (or bake them on a tray in the oven). Set aside to cool.

2. Heat the olive oil in a shallow frying pan while you thinly slice the red onions. Add them to the pan and sweat until soft for a few minutes.

3. Pour the sherry vinegar into the pan, let it sizzle for 10 seconds or so, then crumble in the stock cube and pour in the warm water.

4. Give the onion mixture a gentle stir with a wooden spoon until the sauce begins to thicken, but not so much that it becomes stiff. Turn off the heat and leave the sauce to cool down so it's warm rather than hot, testing it with your finger.

5. Break the crispy ham strips in half and add them to the spinach in the serving bowl. Halve the avocados, remove the stones, scoop out the flesh and slice them vertically. Add to the bowl.

6. Gently pour the warm onion dressing over all the ingredients and gently toss together with your hands, then serve straightaway.

NOTES

If you are a big fan of balsamic vinegar, you can use that instead of the sherry vinegar. As the dressing is savoury and umami, there is no need to add more salt (or pepper) before serving.

SUZY'S CHICKEN MARYLAND SUPREME

In Sydney I had a friend, Suzy, who had a real gift for cooking and taught me a lot about Italian cooking. Pairing chicken with tomatoes, onions, bacon, mushrooms and a good measure of wine and brandy is always a winner. It's also a great substitute for a Sunday roast.

Preparation time: 15 minutes | Cooking time: 1 hour 30 minutes | Serves 2

INGREDIENTS

2 large Chicken Marylands (whole legs, bone-in)

Flour, to coat

Salt and pepper

2 tbsp olive oil

1 large brown onion, diced

1½ carrots, diced

2-3 cloves of garlic, crushed

2 rashers of bacon, diced

2 tbsp tomato purée

2 tbsp Italian passata

Good shake of dried Italian herbs

225ml chicken stock (cubes will do)

225ml white wine (not too dry)

60ml water

2 tbsp brandy

100g large chestnut mushrooms, halved

100g baby potatoes

100g fine green beans

Small handful of fresh mint and parsley, chopped

METHOD

1. Preheat oven to 180°c. Place the chicken legs in a plastic bag with enough flour to coat them. Season with salt and pepper, then seal and shake the bag to coat the chicken evenly.

2. Heat the oil in a casserole dish and fry the chicken legs until golden on all sides. Transfer them to a plate and set aside.

3. Fry the onion, carrots and garlic gently in the residual oil for 2 to 3 minutes. Add the bacon and fry for another 2 to 3 minutes, then stir in the tomato purée, passata and dried herbs.

4. Pour the stock, wine, water and brandy into the casserole and stir thoroughly.

5. Return the chicken to the casserole dish. With a large spoon, pour some of the sauce over the chicken. Cover the dish with a lid and cook in the preheated oven for up to 1 hour 30 minutes (the larger the pieces of chicken, the longer they will need to cook).

6. Check the casserole after 45 minutes. If the sauce is bubbling heavily, turn the oven temperature down to 160°c. Add the mushrooms into the casserole now.

7. Parboil the baby potatoes in a large saucepan of water for 15 minutes. After 12 minutes, add the green beans to cook for the final 3 minutes. Meanwhile, fill a bowl with very cold water.

8. Use a slotted spoon to transfer the cooked beans into the cold water (this keeps them bright green) and drain when cooled.

9. Remove the casserole dish from the oven. Place a chicken leg on each serving plate, add the potatoes and beans, then give the sauce in the casserole a quick stir and spoon some over the chicken. Garnish with the chopped fresh herbs.

NOTES

In Australia, the term 'Chicken Maryland' simply refers to a butcher's cut for a whole leg consisting of the thigh and drumstick. I buy these fresh from the butcher, rather than packaged in the supermarket, as they keep their shape well.

TEX-MEX-ASIAN MASH UP

Mash ups are great for chilly nights when you need spicy and umami foods to keep you warm. This one came about during lockdown, when I couldn't get a food delivery for love nor money, so I chucked a bunch of ingredients from my fridge into a wok and served it with rice!

Preparation time: 10 minutes | Cooking time: 10-15 minutes | Serves 2

INGREDIENTS

100g chorizo, sliced

1 small carrot, sliced

2 baby corn, cut into three chunks

1 shallot, diced

100g fresh beansprouts

90g baby pak choi

4 large chestnut mushrooms, quartered

2 red chillies, deseeded and chopped

2 eggs

150g white rice

2-3 tbsp vegetable oil

30g peanuts

2-3 tbsp light soy sauce

METHOD

1. Divide the prepared ingredients between two bowls: one for the chorizo, carrots, baby corn and shallot, and the other for the beansprouts, pak choi, mushrooms and chillies. Lightly whisk the eggs together in another smaller bowl.

2. Add the rice to a large saucepan and cover with water. Bring to a simmer, then turn the heat down low, cover with a lid and cook for 10 minutes. Turn off the heat, leaving the lid on, and let the rice steam for a further 10 minutes.

3. Meanwhile, put 1 tablespoon of the vegetable oil into a wok over a medium-high heat. Add the whisked eggs and cook while stirring until wobbly but not browning or crisping. Use a slotted spoon to transfer the eggs to a small plate and cut into strips. Set aside.

4. Heat another tablespoon of oil in the wok and throw in the first bowl of ingredients. Stir the mixture for 2 to 3 minutes until lightly cooked.

5. Add the second bowl of ingredients to the wok, stir again (adding the remaining vegetable oil if needed) and cook for another 2 minutes. Toss the peanuts into the mixture towards the end. Splash in 2 tablespoons of the soy sauce and let it bubble up for 30 seconds or so. Stir the mixture, taste to see if the last tablespoon of soy sauce is needed, then turn off the heat.

6. Transfer the rested rice into serving bowls and spoon over the wok mixture. With your fingers, place the egg strips on top and serve immediately.

STRAWBERRY & WALNUT AFTERNOON TEA CAKE

There's a rustic look about this three-tiered cake, so don't make it too neat: let the strawberry cream filling and topping squidge out and slide about a bit. Mum and I baked this all the time when I was a child. Nowadays, I make it for elevenses or afternoon tea with friends.

Preparation time: 30 minutes | Cooking time: 1 hour | Serves 4 or more

INGREDIENTS

225g unsalted butter at room temperature, plus extra for greasing

225g self-raising flour, plus extra for dusting

225g + 1 tbsp golden caster sugar

4 large eggs

100ml milk

2 tbsp coffee extract (I use the Nielsen Massey brand)

50g walnuts, roughly chopped

400g fresh strawberries

300g double cream

METHOD

1. Preheat the oven to 170°c. Grease a deep 20cm springform cake tin with softened butter, then line it with baking paper. Dust the base and sides with flour, tapping off the excess.

2. Place the 225g of butter, flour and sugar into a food processor with the eggs, milk and coffee extract. Blend everything together, then stir in the walnuts with a wooden spoon.

3. Pour the cake mixture into the prepared tin and level the top with a small spatula. Bake in the middle of the preheated oven for 50 to 55 minutes. Do not open the oven for at least the first 30 minutes as the cake may deflate. If a thin skewer comes out clean, it's ready.

4. Turn off the oven but leave the cake inside for 5 to 10 more minutes, with the oven door slightly ajar. Remove the cake from the oven, run a knife around the edge to loosen it from the tin, then leave it to cool for a few minutes before transferring it to a wire rack.

5. Once the cake has cooled completely, use a serrated knife (such as a bread knife) to slice it horizontally into 3 equal layers.

6. Halve 12 strawberries for the topping. Slice the remaining strawberries vertically into 3 pieces each.

7. Using an electric mixer, whip the double cream to soft peaks. Fold the sliced strawberries gently through the cream with a spatula. Divide the cream into thirds, using a knife, to help you end up with even layers of filling.

8. Place the bottom layer of the sponge on a plate or cake stand. Add one third of the strawberry cream, then repeat this process with the middle and top layers, finishing with the last third of strawberry cream. Decorate with the halved strawberries, then slice and serve.

FLAVOURS

The romantic in me wants to believe that flavoursome dishes are a mix of the aromas they produce, the hedonic sensations they trigger and the memories they stir. The rational side of me, however, knows that these dishes are simply a collection of molecules and compounds, with no emotional 'notes.' Yet we gladly choose to take on the alchemist role, turning foods into feasts.

Few dishes are a one-trick pony: even oysters benefit from a friendly companion or two (for example, a wedge of lemon or finely chopped chillies). On the other hand, there is a finite number of flavours that you can include in a single dish. For newcomers to cooking, the best thing is to start with two foods, like a globe artichoke, which you pair with a flavour-friendly food, like lemon or bacon. Combining three to four foods is pairing-plus. Obvious examples include studding a leg of lamb with anchovies, garlic slices and rosemary sprigs.

'Bouncing' is uber-combining, where you start with one food and add another five or six foods that go together. The American chef Grant Achatz is widely recognised as a super-bouncer. One YouTube video in particular is a classic primer for home cooks: he starts with white beans, which go with ham or pancetta, which goes with apples and peas, followed by maple syrup and beer, both of which go with all those other foods.

Some exceptions aside (like raw salads and poke bowls), most flavoursome dishes start with a mix of aromatic foods that you heat in some sort of fat (like butter, oil or coconut milk), which you bring together at the beginning of a dish, like in a casserole or stir-fry. The heated fat helps these ingredients release addictive aromas and impart deep flavours into the dish. When we get into Scents, Condiments and Potions, you'll see how you can add even more flavours to your dishes, but for now let's start with pairing, combining and bouncing your favourite foods.

Getting to grips with flavours
+ Flavour Bases
+ Flavour Families
+ Flavour Cheat Sheets

Flavour Bases are by far the easiest way to experiment with aromas and give you an entry point to take your Go-To and Magical Foods into different cuisines. These will help you get the hang of making flavoursome dishes in a flash.

Culinary traditions are often long established, time-honoured and old. Flavour Bases reflect the various foods, herbs, spices, condiments, oils and dairy products that were available back when food was more localised and you couldn't plant exotic fruit and vegetables in colder climes, nor raise livestock (cattle) and sow crops (wheat grain) in hotter climes. This meant that people cooked dishes with olive oil in southern Europe, while people in northern Europe cooked with butter. Cream turned up in the cooler North, while avocados turned up in the hotter South.

The same applied to fruit: apples, pears and berries were prolific in the North while citrus and stone fruits were dominant in the South (becoming more striking and glamorous the nearer the country was to the equator). Here is a tip for when you are sizing up a recipe: if you are looking at a Normandy chicken casserole, for example, and the ingredients include olive oil, it is not an authentic dish!

Flavour Bases are well understood and easy to create. To clarify, they are not the same as marinades, where you are soaking a food in liquids, herbs, spices and vegetables to bring out or complement the flavour of the main ingredient during the cooking process. While marinades do inject flavours, they are mostly there to soften foods like meat, which benefit from tenderising to retain moisture when cooked.

Set out opposite are a range of Flavour Bases commonly used by chefs and home cooks. For each base, you gather the ingredients for the relevant cuisine. You start by sweating the vegetables with the relevant fat (oil, butter, ghee) until soft. Once the fat bubbles up and the foods turn into a lovely, glossy mix, you lower the heat and add the herbs, spices and liquids (wine, vinegar, coconut milk), then stir. At this point, you add a fast-cooking food to the base, like a fish fillet or some chicken thighs, as you don't want to overcook the base while waiting for the main ingredient to cook. Alternatively, you can transfer the flavour base into a casserole and add a slower-cooking food, like a cut of red meat or a sturdy vegetable such as aubergine.

Shortcuts
Flavour Bases

A French mirepoix, Italian soffritto and Spanish sofrito are all the same thing – a sautéed mixture of vegetables, dried herbs and occasionally pork pieces (chorizo, pancetta).

Flavour Bases

Cajun/Creole
A mix of onion, celery and peppers, with olive oil or butter, supplemented by garlic, parsley, shallots, paprika.

Caribbean
A derivative of a Spanish sofrito, sometimes swapping out olive oil for lard, with the addition of green peppers and sweet chilli peppers. You may also find oregano, coriander and chorizo in Cuban food.

Chinese
A mix of garlic, spring onions and ginger, with cooking oil, supplemented by chillies, shallots, chives, coriander, Chinese five spice, star anise.

French
A mirepoix of onion, carrots and celery, heated in butter, supplemented by basil, parsley, thyme, bay leaves, herbes de Provence.

Italian
A soffritto of onion, carrots and celery, heated in olive oil, supplemented by garlic, basil, fennel, bay leaves, wine, parsley, sage, prosciutto, pancetta.

Indian
A mix of onion, garlic, chillies and ginger and heated in ghee, supplemented by tomatoes, coriander, cardamom, cumin, curry powder/leaves, fenugreek, garam masala, turmeric.

Latin
A mix of garlic, onions, peppers and tomatoes, heated in olive oil, supplemented by chillies, bay leaves, coriander, cumin, paprika, bacon, chorizo, ham, wine, vinegars.

Mexican
Coriander, chillies and garlic, traditionally heated in lard, supplemented by mint, oregano, thyme.

Middle Eastern
A mix of garlic, onions, tomatoes, spring onions and raisins, heated in cooking oil or clarified butter, supplemented by ginger, saffron, turmeric, cinnamon.

Spanish
A sofrito of garlic, onion, paprika and tomatoes, heated in olive oil, supplemented by coriander, chilli, bay leaves.

Thai
Shallots, garlic and chillies, heated in cooking oil or coconut milk, supplemented by basil, coriander, ginger, galangal, kaffir lime, lemongrass.

Unlike Taste Families, where everyone agrees that lemon is sour and rocket is bitter, **Flavour Families** are contested. For example, the common pea is a member of the Green Family in one cook book, but a member of the Grassy and Green Family or Verdant Family in another. Horseradish is either a member of the Mustard Family or the Sulphurous Family, depending on which cook book you're reading.

You might wonder why this is. In short, some chefs cast a wide net, scooping up a range of foods (like berries, citrus fruits, tree fruits) under a large banner, such as a Fruity Family. Other chefs (or writers) might separate those different fruits into Creamy, Fresh and Floral Families. Neither approach is wrong and be assured that no-one thinks peas belong to the Citrus Family nor horseradish to the Marine Family! So don't worry too much about these slightly random labels and focus on the substance instead.

The books I have pored over include *The Flavour Thesaurus* by Niki Segnit, *The Flavor Matrix* by James Briscione and *The Flavor Equation* by Nik Sharma, but there are also excellent websites that focus on the most popular flavour pairings. For ease, I am sharing my ten flavour families on the opposite page. These labels give you a feel for the foods that belong to each family. Listed underneath are typical foods within that family and some suggested pairings with foods in other families. For example, earthy foods like mushrooms go really well with a wide range of citrusy, cheesy, fresh, fruity, nutty and sulphurous foods such as lemons, blue cheese, tomatoes, walnuts, garlic and onions. These pairings are all based on those molecules and compounds that you read about earlier. My list is neither definitive nor exhaustive so it's not perfect, but it might be a good start for you.

Over time, you will find yourself reaching for the right foods instinctively to create all sorts of sumptuous dishes. By far the easiest way to test whether your combinations are going to be successful (though by no means fool-proof!) is to type two or three foods into your preferred search engine and see how many recipes come up. Type in prawns and lemons, and an array of recipes will be at your fingertips. Try prawns and cherries, and you will find... absolutely nada.

Shortcuts
Flavour Families

Cheesy and creamy

Cheesy and creamy family members
Sour milk and cream, alongside the full spectrum of cheeses from mild cheddar to Stinking Bishop.

Pair cheesy and creamy foods with…
Floral, fruity, sulphurous and earthy families.

Citrusy

Citrusy family members
Grapefruits, lemons and oranges from warm regions (Mediterranean, Middle East, Pacific Rim), limes and yuzus from hotter ones (Mexican, Asian).

Pair citrusy foods with…
Earthy, salty and sweet foods.

Earthy

Earthy family members
Root vegetables (beetroots and potatoes), along with aubergine, squashes, celery and mushrooms.

Pair earthy foods with…
Meats. They can also take on both spicy and citrusy flavours (yoghurt, citrus, chillies, capsicums and peppers).

Floral

Floral family members
Orange blossom, rose, lavender, basil, thyme and vanilla.

Pair floral foods with…
Cream, stone and tree fruits, berries and some tropical fruits.

Fruity

Fruity family members
Stone, berry and tree fruits.

Pair fruity foods with…
Apples, pears and stone fruits enjoy vanilla, most nuts, yoghurt, cream and chocolate. Melons, grapes and figs more typically feature in savoury dishes, often paired with salty foods.

Maillard

Maillard family members
A big flavour family covering chocolate, toasted and roasted nuts, meaty and caramelised foods.

Pair maillard foods with…
Has the capacity to carry big flavours (earthy, cheesy, spicy, citrusy and fruity). Less successful with delicate flavours (floral).

Marine

Marine family members
Any food that smells of the sea, such as fish, shellfish and molluscs.

Pair marine foods with…
Citrus fruits and other salty foods (ham, bacon, cheese, olives).

Pungent

Pungent family members
Scents associated with mustardy flavours like watercress, horseradish and wasabi.

Pair pungent foods with…
Beef, oily and white fish and occasionally beetroot.

Spicy

Spicy family members
Covering chillies, capsicums, peppers and parsnips, along with basil, cloves, cinnamon and nutmeg.

Pair spicy foods with…
Wide range of foods, both savoury and sweet.

Sulphurous

Sulphurous family members
Onion family members at one end of the spectrum and cabbages, truffles, swedes, cauliflower and broccoli at the other end.

Pair sulphurous foods with…
Citrusy fruits and toasted nuts, plus eggs.

Once you have a good grasp of Flavour Families and Flavour Bases, you can build up your understanding of pairing, bouncing and combining foods through **Flavour Cheat Sheets**. I routinely update my own Flavour Cheat Sheets, which might seem odd. You might ask why I do this, given the properties of foods haven't really changed over the centuries. While that is true, the culinary world does move forward, discovering new and often unexpected pairings. For example, it turns out that kiwi fruit rather likes sour cranberries. Moreover, it also likes a touch of chilli and coriander. I haven't yet tried this pairing, but I am always interested in new ideas, hence the updates.

On pages 62 and 63 you will find Flavour Cheat Sheets for meat, seafood, vegetables and fruit which you might want to keep somewhere handy for when you're thinking about a dish or special occasion. The first part of the cheat sheet deals with **protein foods**. When getting your combinations right with proteins, what's important is the choice of cooking method:

✦ Dry-heat cooking boosts the caramelisation of surface sugars in foods through pan-frying, searing, roasting, sweating, stir-frying, grilling and baking.

✦ Moist-heat cooking uses water, liquid or steam to transfer heat to foods through poaching, simmering, boiling, braising, stewing and steaming. Vegetables, fruits and grains (pasta, rice, noodles, couscous) sometimes pair differently based on the cooking method.

Next, the cheat sheet deals with the pairing and combinations for **vegetables** in dishes where there is no dominant protein food. This is good for creating appetisers, entrées, sides and salads, and especially useful for pescatarians, vegetarians and vegans.

The last part of the cheat sheet deals with the pairing and combinations for **fruits** in dishes, for whipping up cakes, desserts, puddings and sweets.

I recognise that is a lot of info to take in at one stroke, but if you scan the list and stick it up in your pantry or in one of your cupboards, over time these pairings and combinations will sink in. However, for those of you with a real passion for flavoursome dishes, I came up with a small project for you to engage with now that you have gone through the **foundations of Foods, Tastes and Flavours**. You can find this on page 75.

Shortcuts
Flavour Cheat Sheets

Meat

Beef

Dry veg
Brussels sprouts, carrots, ginger, green beans, horseradish, parsnips, potatoes, sweet potatoes, squashes

Moist veg
Baby corn, beansprouts, pak choi, carrots, cabbage, courgettes, ginger, mushrooms, peppers, sweet potatoes, squashes

Moist grains
Pasta, polenta, rice, noodles, red kidney beans

Chicken

Dry veg
Asparagus, carrots, celery, leeks, potatoes, sweetcorn

Moist veg
Avocado, lettuce, mushrooms, potatoes, spring onions

Moist grains
Pasta, rice, noodles, chickpeas, chilli beans, tortillas

Lamb

Dry veg
Broad beans, carrots, parsnips, peas, potatoes, sweet potatoes, squashes

Moist veg
Aubergine, olives, peppers, potatoes, spinach

Moist grains
Couscous, rice, polenta, chickpeas

Pork

Dry veg
Beetroot, cabbage, celery, ginger, green beans, sweet potatoes

Moist veg
Cabbage, carrots, celery, green beans, sweet potatoes, squashes

Moist grains
Rice, noodles

Seafood

Shellfish
Avocado, chilli, cucumber, fennel, ginger, leeks, peas, potatoes, squashes

Oily fish
Avocado, chilli, cucumber, ginger, green beans, peppers, radishes, spinach

White fish
Carrots, celery, cucumber, green beans, leeks, olives, peppers, potatoes, spinach, spring onions

Pink fish
Asparagus, spring onions, spinach, potatoes

Vegetables

Asparagus
Almonds, hard cheeses, wet cheeses, cream, eggs, hazelnuts, lemon, shallots, tomatoes, yoghurt

Avocado
Cucumbers, limes, spring onions, peppers, rocket, sour cream, sweetcorn, tomatoes, walnuts

Brussels Sprouts
Almonds, blue cheeses, hard cheeses, wet cheeses, chestnuts, cream, hazelnuts, lemons

Beetroot
Apples, hard cheeses, blue cheeses, fennel, lemon, pears, potatoes, radishes, shallots, spinach, walnuts, yoghurt

Broccoli
Almonds, cauliflower, hard cheeses, wet cheeses, garlic, lemon, tomatoes, sweetcorn

Cabbage & Kohlrabi
Apples, carrots, chestnuts, cream, garlic, ginger, potatoes, sour cream

Cauliflower
Broccoli, hard cheeses, blue cheeses, cream, garlic, ginger, pine nuts, tomatoes

Shortcuts
Flavour Cheat Sheets

Carrots
Cream, ginger, lemon, potatoes, spinach, walnuts, yoghurt

Fennel
Almonds, apples, garlic, blue cheeses, lemon, oranges

Alliums
Brussels sprouts, broccoli, cauliflower, lemons

Green Beans
Almonds, hard cheeses, wet cheeses, eggs, garlic, lemons, tomatoes, walnuts

Mushrooms
Almonds, green beans, carrots, blue cheeses, hard cheeses, cream, eggs, garlic, leeks, lemon, peas, shallots, tomatoes, walnuts

Olives
Almonds, soft cheese, garlic, lemon, peppers, pine nuts, spring onions, tomatoes

Potatoes
Chickpeas, cream, hard cheeses, garlic, kale, leeks, lemons, onions, sweetcorn, tomatoes

Peas
Carrots, celery, cream, garlic, leeks, lemon, lettuce, potatoes, shallots, spinach, tomatoes

Peppers
Carrots, soft cheeses, aubergine, garlic, onions, pineapple, potatoes, rocket, spring onions, sweetcorn, squashes

Spinach
Wet cheeses, hard cheeses, cream, eggs, fennel, garlic, pine nuts, tomatoes, walnuts

Sweetcorn
Avocado, carrots, hard cheeses, wet cheeses, cream, garlic, limes, mushrooms, onions, peppers, shallots, sour cream, tomatoes

Squashes
Apples, almonds, blue cheeses, soft cheeses, cranberries, ginger, oranges, pears

Tomatoes
Almonds, carrots, cauliflower, blue cheeses, wet cheeses, cucumbers, aubergines, eggs, garlic, mushrooms, peas, shallots, rocket, sweetcorn, yoghurt

Fruit

Apples
Cranberries, currants, mango, lemons, hazelnuts, walnuts, ginger, hard cheeses, cream, yoghurt

Apricots
Oranges, peaches, plums, almonds, hazelnuts, dark chocolate, pistachios

Bananas
Cherries, limes, mangoes, hazelnuts, dark chocolate, cream

Blackberries
Apricots, lemons, peaches, hazelnuts, cream

Cherries
Apricots, peaches, plums, dark chocolate, walnuts

Figs
Almonds, apples, blue cheeses, soft cheeses, grapes, lemons, pistachios, raspberries, rocket, walnuts

Lemons & Limes
Apricots, peaches, nectarines, plums, ginger, dark chocolate, white chocolate, almonds, pistachios

Mangoes & Papayas
Apples, melon, limes, pomegranates

Oranges
Figs, cranberries, red berries, blackberries, dark chocolate

Peaches & Nectarines
Oranges, lemons, limes, blackberries, pistachios, almonds, hazelnuts

Pears
Apples, lemons, almonds, hazelnuts, walnuts, dark chocolate, hard cheeses, cream

Plums
Lemons, limes, almonds, hazelnut, cream

Raspberries
Lemons, peaches, apricots, ginger, white chocolate, cream

Rhubarb
Apples, apricots, peaches, strawberries, ginger, almonds, cream

Strawberries
Apples, lemons, rhubarb, almonds, hazelnuts, dark chocolate, white chocolate, cream

My journey with flavours

Before the Internet, if you wanted to learn something new you had to go to a bookshop to find the relevant reference/handbook/instruction manual. What I wanted at that time was a magical book that could tell me why I loved my recipe for sizzled prawns with chorizo or why I had never seen a recipe in which prawns were paired with a raspberry sauce.

Of all the challenges I set myself on the road to my magical kitchen, understanding Flavour Bases and Flavour Families was unquestionably the most demanding as a non-professional cook. These days, bloggers, magazine articles, cooking writers and chefs do a great job of helping us with the 'why' behind flavours, using vivid descriptors. For example, pork dishes can contain 'tantalising combinations of woodland and farmyard flavours' while almonds and lamb can be a 'luxurious pairing'. Monkfish can be 'sweet and buttery, a little shellfish-y without the full butter-kissed-popcorn flavour of prawns' and white chocolate 'emphasises raspberries' sharpness and perfumed flavour' while dark chocolate 'used in moderation adds richness and depth to savoury dishes' (think Mexican mole). Sometimes, I roll my eyes when recipes sink into purple prose, but in truth I have learnt from them all.

To this day, I remain convinced of two things when it comes to pairing, combining and bouncing flavours. First, we don't come out of our mother's womb knowing this stuff. Second, we can up our game without having to know every possible pairing and combination on the planet, because there is no benefit to learning about foods that go best with shellfish if shellfish is not one of your Go-To Foods!

My **Stardust Tip** is to begin your flavour journey with starters: soups, salads, sides, sharing plates. It will be easier for you to experiment with these smaller dishes before you build up to full-blown main courses. Don't worry about the science behind flavour pairing and bouncing. Kick off with the classic combinations. Over time, not only will the science fall into place, but so will the art! In the meantime, when you have some time on your hands, go crazy in your magical kitchen. Rip up the rulebook and come up with some of your own flavour pairings. No one will be watching and, who knows, maybe you'll come up with something simply spectacular like maple bacon ice cream!

See the following pages for recipes that show you how to pair and combine foods for flavour.

I'm a firm believer that the world should be your oyster when you're cooking. People should open themselves to other cuisines - there are a lot of hidden secrets all over the world.

Yotam Ottolenghi

JACKET SCALLOPS

A retro classic and one of my mum's favourites. This dish seemed to disappear for a couple of decades, giving way to more Asian-influenced flavours with seafood. I still like it as a wintry comfort food, served in scallop shells with a bubbling, golden topping.

Preparation time: 10 minutes | Cooking time: 20 minutes | Serves 2

INGREDIENTS

For the crumb topping

3 tbsp panko breadcrumbs

2 tbsp chopped fresh parsley

1 tbsp grated Gruyère

1 tbsp cold butter

Salt and pepper

For the scallops

4 large scallops, cleaned (no roe) with shells

2 peppercorns

1 bay leaf

1 tsp lemon juice

For the sauce

1 tbsp butter

1 small stick of celery, finely diced

1 small leek, finely diced

50ml white wine

2 tbsp double cream

METHOD

1. For the crumb topping, whizz the panko breadcrumbs and parsley in a food processor until green. Add the cheese and butter, then whizz again until combined but still crumbly. Season to taste with salt and pepper, then set aside.

2. For the scallops, place the cleaned scallops in a medium saucepan of cold water. Add the peppercorns, bay leaf and lemon juice. Poach for 5 minutes over a medium heat, then transfer the scallops to a plate.

3. For the sauce, melt the butter in a shallow frying pan over a medium heat. Add the celery and leek and cook for 3 to 4 minutes, or until the vegetables are soft.

4. Add the white wine and cream to the pan for the sauce and let the mixture bubble for 5 minutes, turning down the heat if the vegetables start to brown.

5. Place the poached scallops on the shells, cover them with the sauce, then scatter over a generous helping of the crumb topping.

6. Place the filled shells over every other hole in a muffin tin. This stops them wobbling and spilling over while cooking. Brown the jacket scallops under the grill for 3 minutes or so, until golden and bubbling, then serve hot.

NOTES

This goes well with a side salad of soft lettuce with a lemony vinaigrette. You can find cleaned scallop shells at the fishmonger or buy them online.

PEANUT & MISO PORK STIR-FRY

My first visit to a Benihana restaurant was in Hawaii, of all places. I was clueless about Japanese food and daunted by the menu, but immediately fell in love with the delicate, mildly sweet flavour of shiro (white) miso. It's always in my pantry for making stir-fries with.

Preparation time: 20 minutes | Cooking time: 10 minutes | Serves 2

INGREDIENTS

For the sauce

2 tbsp smooth peanut butter

2 tbsp white miso paste

2 tbsp lime juice

1 tsp vegetable oil

1 tsp red chilli flakes

For the stir-fry

200g pork tenderloin

1 tbsp vegetable oil

150g dried noodles

½ pointed cabbage, finely shredded

½ red cabbage, finely shredded

1 large carrot, cut into batons

1 tbsp soy sauce

200g choi sum (leaves only)

Lime wedges, to serve

METHOD

1. For the sauce, combine the peanut butter and miso in a bowl with a fork, then stir in the lime juice, vegetable oil and chilli flakes. Add a little cool water to the paste and mix until it has the consistency of double cream. Set aside.

2. Dice the pork into 3cm cubes while you heat the oil in a wok (or large frying pan) over a high heat. Stir-fry the cubed pork in the hot oil for 6 minutes, until browned and caramelised. Meanwhile, cook the noodles according to the instructions on the packet.

3. Add both types of cabbage to the wok and stir-fry for 2 to 3 minutes. Add the carrot, cooked noodles and soy sauce to fry for a further 2 to 3 minutes. add the choi sum leaves and stir-fry for 1 to 2 minutes.

4. Make sure the pork is cooked by removing a cube from the wok and cutting it in half to check the meat is no longer pink.

5. Pour the peanut and miso sauce into the wok and incorporate it using a wooden spoon. Divide the stir-fry between two bowls and add a few lime wedges to squeeze over the dish.

NOTES

Choi sum is slightly more robust than pak choi and slightly more bitter, which works with the flavours in this dish. You can add a sprinkle of chopped fresh coriander at the end if you're keen, but there's quite a lot going on in this dish already. A better option would be sliced spring onions.

SEARED STEAK WITH BROAD BEANS & LEMONY YOGHURT DRESSING

I prefer to serve sirloin steaks hot, straight from the cast-iron griddle pan. Lemon isn't a classic flavour pairing for a steak dish, but it works beautifully in the dressing for the side of broad beans. You can buy preserved lemons, but I have included an easy homemade version here.

Preparation time: 1 hour, plus 24 hours preserving | Cooking time: 15 minutes | Serves 2

INGREDIENTS

For the preserved lemons

8 medium-large lemons

50g sea salt

For the garnish

2 shallots, sliced

2 tbsp safflower oil

1 tsp salt

1 tsp nigella seeds

For the broad beans

300g broad beans

1 tbsp olive oil

For the dressing

60g crème fraîche

60g thick natural yoghurt

1 clove of garlic, peeled and grated

1 tsp cracked black pepper

For the steaks

2 sirloin steaks

1 tsp each salt and pepper

1 tbsp safflower oil

METHOD

1. Start the preserved lemons 24 hours before you want to serve the dish. Quarter the lemons, rub the sea salt into them, place in a bowl and cover with cold water. Make the bowl airtight with cling film. Set aside for 12 hours at room temperature to cure, then move them into the fridge for another 12 hours until chilled.

2. The following day, remove the steaks from the fridge 1 hour before serving. Preheat the oven to 120°c and toss the sliced shallots with the safflower oil and salt. Spread them on a baking tray and cook in the preheated oven for about 20 minutes, turning occasionally, until golden and crisp.

3. Meanwhile, fill a large bowl with ice and cold water and set aside. Bring a large pan of salted water to the boil, add the broad beans and blanch them until they are bright green (2 to 3 minutes). Transfer the beans straight into the iced water to cool.

4. Now make the dressing. Bring together the crème fraîche, yoghurt, grated garlic and cracked black pepper in a medium bowl. Taste and season with salt as needed, then dice the chilled preserved lemons and add them to the dressing.

5. Drain the cooled broad beans and pat dry with some kitchen towel. Toss the beans in the tablespoon of olive oil to give them some gloss. Set aside in a cool place.

6. Pat your steaks as dry as you can with some kitchen towel, then season them on both sides with the salt and pepper. Heat the griddle pan for a few minutes, using a small brush to coat it thinly with the safflower oil. Lay the steaks into the hot pan and sear for 3 to 4 minutes on each side, until browned on the outside and medium rare. Transfer the steaks to a plate, cover with tin foil and let them rest for 5 minutes.

7. Plate the rested steaks. Add the broad beans and cover them with a generous helping of the lemony yoghurt dressing, then scatter with the crispy shallots and nigella seeds.

NOTES

I recommend investing in a heavy griddle pan for cooking vegetables, fish and meat. Grill marks create a flavourful crust and the ridges let the food cook above any rendered fat.

CHOCOLATE ORANGE & CHILLI TART

I like to serve this tart with caramelised orange slices to complement the citrus in the filling. The chilli is optional, but if you've tried it with chocolate you'll know it's a heavenly combination. Feel free to make your own sweet pastry, but there's no shame in using a quality shop-bought tart case.

Preparation time: 2 hours | Cooking time: 40 minutes | Serves 4

INGREDIENTS

250ml double cream

1 tbsp fresh orange zest

$\frac{1}{4}$ tsp chilli flakes (optional)

200g dark chocolate (I like Callebaut chocolate drops)

20g unsalted butter, softened

1 shop-bought sweet pastry case

For the caramelised orange slices

100g golden caster sugar

2 oranges, sliced

$\frac{1}{2}$ tsp fresh thyme leaves

METHOD

1. Put the cream and orange zest into a large saucepan over a medium heat and bring to a simmer. Remove from the heat and stir in the chilli flakes, if using. Cover with cling film and leave in a warm place to infuse for 30 minutes.

2. Put the chocolate and butter in a heatproof glass bowl and rest it over a saucepan of gently simmering water, making sure the bottom of the bowl does not touch the water. Heat for 3 to 5 minutes over a low heat until the chocolate has melted, stirring frequently with a spatula and making sure no water gets into the bowl.

3. Strain the cream through a fine sieve to discard the orange zest and chilli flakes. Pour the infused cream very slowly into the chocolate mixture while you whisk with an electric handheld mixer on a medium speed until the filling is soft and shiny.

4. Pour the chocolate filling into the pastry case and set aside in a cool place (but not the fridge) for 1 hour 30 minutes until just set.

5. While the filling is setting, make the caramelised orange slices. You can make these with blood oranges when they are in season. Put the sugar in a medium saucepan with 300ml of water and bring to the boil. Add the sliced oranges and boil gently for about 15 to 20 minutes, or until the orange peel is starting to turn translucent.

6. Reduce the heat to a gentle simmer and cook the oranges for another 10 to 15 minutes, or until the liquid has reduced to a thick syrup. Remove the slices from the pan and place on a baking tray lined with baking paper, then leave to cool completely.

7. When the tart is ready to serve, slice with a sharp knife and plate. Transfer the caramelised orange slices to the plates using a metal spatula and sprinkle them with the thyme leaves.

NOTES

If you are using a large chocolate bar instead of drops, chop it into uniform pieces so it melts evenly. It's important to melt the chocolate slowly over a low heat to avoid it becoming lumpy or grainy, and to avoid all contact with water.

Congrats for getting to this point; now is the perfect time to give yourself a well-deserved pat on the back. You can pause your journey here or you can continue onto the next three steps: how to use herbs and spices, condiments and alcohol in cooking. Ahead of that, let's go through your recipes and see how they stack up against your Go-To and Magical Foods. Depending on how many recipes you have, this might take a good couple of hours. Feel free to bring out your favourite bevvy for this!

Do This

Magical Recipes

You will need: 100 index cards plus your cook books, recipe folders and scrapbooks and any recipes you've stored on your laptop, tablet or phone.

Start

Take 50 index cards to begin with. Pick one of your Magical Foods (e.g. chocolate) and write 'Chocolate' on the top left or right of the card as you wish. Repeat this with all of your Magical Foods. Then spread the cards out on a flat surface (kitchen bench, table, carpet or floor).

Sort

Take each recipe one by one and write down the title of it (for example, Tuna Ceviche) on the appropriate card based on the main ingredient (which would be tuna, in this case). Where there is no main ingredient in the recipe (e.g. a tomato, avocado and mozzarella salad), pick out the food that you love most (e.g. avocado) and add it to the appropriate card. When you come across recipes that do not feature one of your Magical Foods, put these aside.

Reflect and review

Add up the number of recipes you have for each of your Magical Foods. Then create two piles of your cards: one for cards where you listed five or more recipes, the other for those where you listed less than five recipes. Lastly, tot up the number of recipes you have that do not feature any of your Magical Foods.

Make some notes for yourself:

Are you light on recipes for some of your MFs? If so, are they really your MFs? Alternatively, have you just not yet found any good recipes for them?

Are you binging big time on just a few of your MFs? If so, can you let some of the recipes go, in order to make way for others?

If you have a lot of recipes that don't include any of your MFs, is it worth taking another look at them? It's not too late to tweak your list and may open up new horizons for you.

All done? Sit back and take a break.

FIXTURES

SCENTS

If anything brings out the obsessive-compulsive in the home cook, it's herbs, spices and blends: aka Scents. From anise to za'atar and any number of household names in between, the world of scents beguiles, intoxicates and delights. You'll want to make the most of these aromatic beauties to complement your Go-To and Magical Foods.

However, you don't need *every* scent under the sun. While you may not yet be in what I call Imelda Marcos territory (the former First Lady of the Philippines, who had a serious addiction to shoes: 3,000 pairs and counting...), you probably have far more herbs and spices than is really necessary. My scents collection tops out at around 25, depending on the season (more in the autumn and winter when I am baking and need a wide range of spices, and less in spring and summer when I exchange warmer, musky spices for delicate, fresh and fragrant herbs).

The words we use to describe the effects of scents are similar to those that fashionistas use, such as boost, elevate, infuse, lift and perk up. I think of scents as the culinary equivalent of touching up an otherwise simple, but classic, get up (crisp white shirt, leather jacket), with a kick-ass accessory or two (funky scarf, Panama hat). Some of us are better than others at picking the perfect piece to complement different outfits, and I think the same can be said of scents. Which scents to choose and when to use them in various regional cuisines is not something you just know, but something you learn.

Scents are the first of the three 'fittings' covered in this book. The other two are condiments and alcohol. I call these Co-With Foods. They are different from Go-To Foods in three aspects: none of them are worth eating on their own (anyone for cinnamon bark?); many are the beating heart of a particular cuisine (chilli for Mexican, dill for Nordic); and some link to specific dishes (like Dijon mustard for steak frites).

Getting to grips with scents

+ Scent Bunches
+ Scent Capsules
+ Using Scents in Cooking

Scent Bunches are like-minded herbs and spices that follow the contours of nature (herbs) and trade routes (spices). If you were on your hols in Prague, strolling through one of the open-air markets, you would come across large bunches of fresh dill, marjoram, mint and parsley along with sachets of allspice, caraway and paprika, which go into popular Czech dishes like goulash, schnitzel and pork roasts. Should you travel due south for 600 miles, however, finishing up in Naples, you would be met with the sweet smells of basil, oregano, thyme and tarragon along with saffron, coriander and chillies which appear in many a pizza, pasta and risotto.

Different countries and continents are host to different types of scents. Broadly, then:

- ✦ Cooler northern and eastern European bunches include herby dill, bay leaves, caraway, chives, celery, mint, parsley, horseradish and spicy cinnamon, ginger, nutmeg, allspice, saffron and white pepper, plus paprika the further east you go.

- ✦ Warmer southern and Mediterranean bunches include herby mint, oregano, basil, thyme, tarragon, rosemary, sage, fennel, lavender and spicy saffron, coriander and paprika, plus chillies the further south you go, and sumac, baharat and za'atar the further east you go.

- ✦ Temperate North American and warmer South American bunches track with European bunches. Fiery (Mexican) epazote, peppers and chillies are used liberally the more southern you go.

- ✦ The enormous expanse of Asia makes it impossible to follow a single rule. Spicy chillies and ginger are fairly universal but after that, you have to drill into regional cuisines: herby Vietnamese mint, Thai basil, Japanese shichimi togarashi, Chinese Szechuan peppercorns and five spice. Tropical Indian bunches are dominated by spicy chillies, coriander, turmeric, cumin, ginger, garam masala, panch phoran, anise, cardamom, saffron and cloves, with a few select herbs (mostly mint).

Like the Taste Families we looked at earlier, which *were not* contested, while Flavour Families *were* contested, the same goes for scents. Everyone agrees that herby oregano is a member of the Mint family (objective), but spicy cumin may be considered a member of one or other of an Aromatic or Warm family (subjective). I wouldn't work yourself up about this, but if it helps, I think Sophie Grigson's book, *Spices*, has the most intuitive approach to spice families. Worth a read if you're into spicy foods.

One major difference between herbs and spices is this: herbs come both dry and fresh, while most spices just come dried. Many home cooks fret about using dried herbs, especially when they're also available fresh. In my view, it is better to have dried herbs in your kitchen – for back up, if no other reason – than to have no herbs at all.

I have a hunch that many home cooks are much better at picking out which spices to use in cooking, rather than herbs. Maybe it's because spices feature heavily in cookery programmes, where TV chefs are dashing about in faraway places. Or maybe we just love the look and feel of spices, like scrolls of cinnamon bark, knobbly chunks of ginger and star-cut anise.

Are spices more interesting than herbs? For sure, there are more cook books on spices than there are on herbs. In their favour is the number of savoury and sweet dishes to which they can contribute. Spices also have long shelf lives. On the other hand, herbs are easier to work with. I'm always happy when snipping away at a vigorous bay tree or a sprawling oregano plant, which feels much more tactile than opening a jar. Despite some limitations, I think herbs can kick arse along with the best spices when used in the right way.

Scent Capsules help you choose which scents you will want to include in your kitchen for the type of dishes and cuisines you favour. Scents tend to find their way into all sorts of nooks and crannies; spices move around in cupboards, dried herbs often find themselves next to vinegars and mustards, while fresh herbs wander between windowsills and vegetable containers in the fridge. Keeping all your scents together makes meal prep much easier, but how to organise them isn't that easy.

One evening on the train home, while reading an article on 'capsule wardrobes', I stumbled on an idea for organising my herbs and spices. If scents were the culinary equivalent of sprucing up an outfit, then why not come up with a 'scent capsule' collection? Rather than focus on which scents went with which foods, I used an approach based on the three key principles for building up a capsule clothes wardrobe: routine (everyday things like coats and jackets), flexible (items that go with at least other three pieces) and limited (special occasions only). I translated those principles to the world of scents:

- ✦ **Routine** – scents that go with your Magical Foods
- ✦ **Flexible** – scents that would go with your favourite cuisines
- ✦ **Limited** – scents you need for one or two sensational dishes you love to make

Following this approach, I ended up with three sets of herbs and spices that I would always stock in my kitchen:

- ✦ Routine – rosemary, basil, tarragon, thyme, coriander, parsley (herbs) and black pepper, saffron, paprika, vanilla (spices)
- ✦ Flexible – marjoram, oregano, chives, kaffir lime leaves, mint (herbs) and chillies, nutmeg, mixed spice, cardamom, cumin, cloves (spices)
- ✦ Limited – Kashmiri chilli powder for Rick Stein's recipe for pan-fried mackerel fish fry; lemongrass for one of my favourite Asian soups; and wasabi for sushi nights

From that point on, I had three different-sized containers for my scents, which were easy to pull out of my cupboards when I was prepping for a meal. There are many ways to sort your scents and if you have a good system going for you, I wouldn't suggest you change it. However, do have a think about how well it's working now that you have identified your Go-To and Magical Foods.

Using scents in cooking is all about **layering.** In short, we use scents to add depth of flavour to our dishes. A tasty dish built on foods that go together can be perfect in its own right, but add a few herbs and spices, and you will have a more complex and satisfying dish. You don't have to be a professional chef to understand the basics of flavour layering. Forget the label and focus on the endgame: adding different, but complementary, flavours to a dish to create depth beyond the original, raw ingredients. You can layer for taste and for flavour with proteins, vegetables, fruits, grains, dairy products and nuts, but when you add scents, you go up a layer.

I have set out some dishes that certain herbs go best with, and with which they are usually associated. More often than not, only one herb is included in a dish, as you can see below. Tabbouleh is a good example of a dish where there are lots of herbs (parsley, mint and sometimes coriander) but it is an exception to the rule. I have taken a different approach for spices. There are some sweet recipes that call for a single spice, like nutmeg in a rice pudding, but when it comes to savoury recipes, it's more usual to have a large range of spices included. Therefore, I've given some examples of regional spice blends and what they are usually made up of. The examples given here are neither exhaustive nor comprehensive, but they should give you a feel for how scents are used in cooking and which scents you might want to have in your kitchen.

Northern and Eastern European Dishes

Herby

+ Parsley – parsley sauces, Dover sole, baked cod, moules marinière (mussels)
+ Dill – dill sauces, potato salads, gravadlax (marinated salmon)
+ Rosemary – lamb, chicken and game dishes
+ Sage – stuffing, pork meatballs and schnitzel, sausages
+ Thyme – baked fish, pâtés and terrines, roasted carrots
+ Mint – peas, roast lamb
+ Chives – white fish fillets, egg dishes, potato salads
+ Horseradish – red meats (especially beef) and oily fish (tuna, smoked trout)

Spicy

+ Mixed spice – British blend of sweet spices which usually contains allspice, cinnamon, cloves, coriander, ginger and nutmeg
+ Quatre épices – French four spice mix which usually comprises pepper, cloves, nutmeg and ginger

Warmer Southern European Dishes

Herby

+ Basil – pesto, caprese, panzanella (Tuscan salad), minestra verde (Italian soup)
+ Dill – white fish fillets, pastas, Greek orzo salad
+ Fennel – mayonnaise, creamy sauces
+ Tarragon – béarnaise sauce
+ Marjoram – pizza, grilled lamb racks
+ Oregano – aubergine dishes
+ Rosemary – chicken and lamb dishes, focaccia
+ Sage – calf's liver and veal, sage butter sauces
+ Thyme – ratatouille
+ Mint – tzatziki, feta salads
+ Bay leaves – beef and lamb casseroles, pâtés and terrines

Spicy

+ Vadouvan – French derivative of an Indian masala curry blend usually containing cumin, turmeric, cardamom, curry leaves, black mustard and fenugreek
+ Adobo – Mexican or Filipino sauce often containing oregano, salt and black pepper
+ Bouillabaisse base – the foundations of a French stew using saffron and star anise

Middle Eastern and Persian Dishes

Herby

✦ Coriander – kebabs, meatballs, stir-fries, salads

✦ Mint – tabbouleh, fruit salads

✦ Parsley – salt-cod fritters

✦ Basil – cherry tomato couscous salads, watermelon salads

✦ Rosemary – chicken dishes

Spicy

✦ Ras el hanout – complex spice blend found in Tunisia, Algeria and Morocco, often including rose petals and lavender flowers

✦ Dhana jeera – West Indian blend of toasted cumin and coriander seeds

✦ Za'atar – Middle Eastern mix of sumac, thyme, sesame seeds and salt

✦ Baharat – another Middle Eastern blend usually containing black pepper, coriander, cinnamon, cloves, cumin, cardamom, nutmeg and paprika

✦ Dukkah – Egyptian seasoning containing sesame seeds, coriander, cumin, salt and black pepper

Indian and Southeast Asian Dishes

Herby

✦ Curry leaves – added whole to curries

✦ Coriander – curries, dhals, chutneys

✦ Mint – Thai soups, curries

✦ Lemongrass – soups, casseroles, curries

✦ Kaffir lime leaves – used in many Thai, Indonesian, Malaysian, Burmese and Vietnamese dishes

Spicy

✦ Tandoori masala – garam masala, garlic, ginger, onion and cayenne pepper

✦ Chinese five spice – Szechuan peppercorns, star anise, cinnamon, fennel seeds and ginger

✦ Shichimi togarashi – Japanese seven spice blend including Szechuan peppercorns, sesame seeds, chilli, dried nori, orange peel and black poppy seeds

✦ Sri Lankan curry powder – coriander seeds, cumin seeds, fennel seeds, cinnamon, cloves, cardamom pods, bay leaves and chillies

✦ Pho – Vietnamese noodle soup with a broth containing star anise, whole cloves, cinnamon sticks, cardamom pods and coriander seeds

For those of you who have a sweet tooth, or simply love baking, likely contenders in your kitchen include **aromatic, warm, sweet** and **scented spices** such as allspice, cacao nibs, cardamom, chilli (great with chocolate), cinnamon, cloves, ground coriander, cumin, ginger, mace, nutmeg, star anise and vanilla (this works with almost every dessert).

My journey with scents

In my mum's kitchen, you could count the number of fresh herbs she had on one hand: bitter curly parsley, mild chives, lemony-piney rosemary and earthy sage. Pots of basil, tarragon, coriander and oregano – which you and I might consider essentials – were simply unobtainable. In the spring, she sowed some of the more delicate herbs (dill, fennel, chervil) but rarely did they fulfil their potential. There were many dishes that she could not cook out of season for lack of fresh herbs, whereas now everyone can buy them from famers' markets and supermarkets.

Less challenging for mum and I back in the day were spices. Given that I was the Dessert to her Main, I spent more time cooking with spices than herbs, and by extension, I was more comfortable adding spices to savoury dishes. That said, it took longer for me to engage with some of the more exotic spices available to us, and to learn how to pair them with my Magical and Go-To Foods. Yet again, what sped up my understanding was reading recipe books, watching cookery programs and travelling to other countries, where I experienced first-hand the various aromas that spices generate: fiery, pungent, musky, nutty, spicy, sweet and sharp.

I have made more mistakes using spices in savoury dishes than I have in sweet dishes. In the beginning, I pulled my punches in the kitchen. If a recipe asked for two tablespoons of caraway seeds, I would only add one tablespoon, just to be on the safe side. Little by little, however, I became more courageous – accepting what seemed to me an excess of spices in the various recipes I tried – which led me to appreciate how amazing scents are.

It does take time to find which scents you like most, but the more you try them, the more you will know which aromas they produce, and whether they go with your favourite foods. As your confidence grows, you will find yourself creating your own dishes (or at least tweaking other people's recipes!).

My **Stardust Tip** for scents is to choose a shelf or drawer where you can easily see your Scent Capsules placed in those three containers I mentioned before. Fresh herbs are best stored in the fridge; wrap them in a damp paper towel and pop them in a paper (or plastic) bag to extend their fridge-life. Lastly, note that scents appear cheap when compared to other foods, but when you have upwards of 25, you are making a reasonable investment, so do cook with them regularly.

Off we go then, with a few fragrant recipes packed with herbs and spices.

Cooking at home with fresh ingredients means you know what's going into your food.
Joe Wicks

POSH MUSHROOMS ON TOAST

This is a great one-pan starter: creamy, garlicy mushrooms with thyme and a cheeky glug of white wine, served on your favourite toast. If that wasn't enough, it's also vegan friendly and you can easily scale up the recipe to make enough for a luscious lunch.

Preparation time: 10 minutes | Cooking time: 15 minutes | Serves 2

INGREDIENTS

150-200g mushrooms (use your favourite variety)

50g plant-based butter or spread

2 cloves of garlic, finely sliced

Salt and pepper, to taste

6 sprigs of fresh thyme, leaves picked

50ml dry white wine

200ml plant-based cream (I used Elmlea Plant)

2 slices of good bread (I like to use a French boule)

Rocket, to serve

METHOD

1. Clean your mushrooms with kitchen towel. Do not wash them as there is more than enough moisture in the mushrooms already! Slice or tear the mushrooms into bite-size pieces, remembering that mushrooms shrink by half when cooked.

2. Place a large non-stick frying pan on the hob on a medium-high heat. Start cooking the butter and garlic straightaway.

3. Add the mushrooms when the butter starts to sizzle, tossing them in the pan to evenly coat in the butter. Season with lots of pepper.

4. Once the mushrooms start to brown (this should take 2 to 3 minutes) add the thyme leaves to the pan and toss again.

5. Now pour in the wine but be careful as the pan may spit. This will add flavour to the mushroom sauce as well as deglazing the pan. Allow the wine to cook away completely, then add the cream and reduce the heat to medium.

6. Leave the sauce to thicken, stirring occasionally, for about 5 minutes. In the meantime, toast your bread.

7. Give your mushrooms one final taste and season with salt and extra pepper if needed. Place the toast on your serving plates, spoon over the mushrooms and sauce, then top with a little fresh rocket.

NOTES

For a fancier presentation when you want to impress, cut the toast on the diagonal and place one piece on top of the other at an angle. You can also rub the cut side of half a garlic clove over the hot toast for an extra kick, and/or sprinkle some lemon zest over the mushrooms for a bit of zing.

MARINATED TOFU WITH FRAGRANT NOODLES

This simple vegan meal uses tofu as a source of protein and to carry gorgeous Asian flavours through the dish. The fragrant noodles are packed with herbs and spices, creating amazing aromas. It takes a bit of time to prep, but it's worth every second!

Preparation time: 1 hour | Cooking time: 15 minutes | Serves 2

INGREDIENTS

For the marinated tofu

300g block of firm tofu (I use the Sainsbury's Organic Super Firm brand)

2 tbsp (30ml) dark soy sauce

2 tbsp (30ml) sesame oil

2 tbsp (30ml) rice wine vinegar

2 tbsp (30ml) runny honey

2 cloves of garlic, grated

10g fresh root ginger, grated

Black pepper, to taste

2 tbsp stir-fry oil

For the fragrant noodles

Bunch of spring onions

20g fresh coriander

20g Thai basil

1 chilli, deseeded

1 red pepper, deseeded

2 cloves of garlic, grated

10g fresh root ginger, grated

1 lime, zested and juiced

1 tbsp light soy sauce

1 tbsp sesame oil

2 nests of medium rice noodles

METHOD

1. For the marinated tofu, first line a container with a double layer of kitchen towel. Remove the tofu from its packaging, gently squeezing out the water as you do, and place the tofu into the lined container, then cover it with more kitchen towel. Place another container holding 3 full tins on top of the tofu.

2. Leave the tofu to press for 30 minutes. You may need to change the kitchen towel halfway through as it soaks up the liquid. Meanwhile, combine all the remaining ingredients except the stir-fry oil in a bowl to make the marinade and leave this to rest.

3. For the fragrant noodles, finely slice the spring onions, discarding the roots and very tops. Finely chop the herbs, chilli and red pepper. Put them all in a bowl with the grated garlic and ginger, lime zest and juice, soy sauce and sesame oil.

4. Carefully slice the block of pressed tofu in half horizontally to give you two long slices (as if you were splitting a cake to fill) and cut these into bite-size cubes. Add the cubed tofu to the marinade, turning it gently to coat each piece, then cover and place in the fridge to rest for at least 30 minutes.

5. Heat the stir-fry oil in a wok over a medium-high heat while you drain the chilled tofu, keeping any leftover marinade. Add the tofu to the wok and stir-fry for about 5 to 8 minutes, gently tossing occasionally to cook the cubes evenly.

6. Cook the rice noodles according to the instructions on the packet, then drain immediately and toss in a spoonful of sesame oil to stop them sticking together. Combine the noodles with the fragrant herb mixture. Cover to prevent it drying out.

7. Add any leftover marinade to the wok with a splash of water to create a light sauce. Serve the tofu on top of the fragrant noodles, drizzled with the sauce from the wok. Squeeze over a little extra lime juice if you fancy a bit more zing!

NOTES

You can add some sliced mushrooms, spring onions and peppers to the wok with the tofu in Step 5 to bulk out the dish if you like.

RACK OF LAMB WITH SPICY MINT SALSA & BABY POTATOES

I love a rack of lamb. The meat needs to be tender and not overcooked, so do invest in a small meat thermometer. Searing the lamb in a frying pan and then transferring it to the oven generally works well. I've paired this with a herby, spicy salsa for extra flavour.

Preparation time: 5-10 minutes | Cooking time: 15 minutes | Serves 2

INGREDIENTS

150g baby potatoes

2 tbsp olive oil

1 rack of lamb (3-4 ribs per person)

For the salsa

100g fresh mint, finely chopped

30g fresh French parsley, finely chopped

2 anchovy fillets in oil, drained and finely chopped

$\frac{1}{2}$ tbsp rinsed and drained capers, finely chopped

$\frac{1}{2}$ clove of garlic, finely chopped

$\frac{1}{4}$ tsp crushed red chilli flakes

150ml olive oil

1 tsp Dijon mustard

Salt and pepper

Dash of lemon juice (optional)

METHOD

1. Preheat the oven to 190°c. For the salsa, combine the herbs, anchovies, capers, garlic and chilli flakes in a bowl. Slowly pour in the olive oil while stirring with a fork. Add the Dijon mustard and stir again, then season with salt and pepper to taste. If the salsa is very spicy, add a dash of lemon juice.

2. Bring a large saucepan of water to the boil over a medium-high heat. Add the baby potatoes and cook for 12 to 15 minutes. Turn the heat down low towards the end, when the lamb is cooked and resting.

3. While the potatoes are cooking, place a large frying pan over a high heat and rub the olive oil over the rack of lamb, then season it with salt and pepper. Sear the rack in the hot pan fat-side down for about 2 minutes, until golden brown. Turn it over with tongs and sear on the other side for 1 minute.

4. Transfer the lamb to a wire rack and place in the preheated oven on a baking tray. Insert a small meat thermometer into one of the meatier ribs in the centre.

5. Cook the lamb until the internal temperature reaches 70°c. This should take between 6 and 8 minutes, depending on your oven.

6. Remove the lamb from the oven, cover with foil and rest for at least 5 minutes before carving and serving with the baby potatoes and spicy mint salsa.

NOTES

No matter how finely I chop the fresh herbs, I often end up with a chunky mint salsa. If that happens, I pop the mixture into my NutriBullet and give it a few blasts to make the salsa finer: not the consistency of single cream, but somewhere in the middle.

SPICED HAM WITH PEACH COUSCOUS

Gammon joints thrive with a thick and piquant glaze using warm and hot spices. They also go well with fruity foods, like peaches, and the nutty sweetness of couscous. Although it takes time, the ham is the only thing that needs cooking here and the leftovers are so versatile.

Preparation time: 15 minutes | Cooking time: 1 hour 15 minutes | Serves 2

INGREDIENTS

½ onion, grated

60g brown sugar

1 tbsp sea salt

1 tsp cayenne

½ tsp black pepper

½ tsp sweet paprika

750g smoked boneless gammon joint

For the peach couscous

80g couscous

1 large ripe peach, destoned and diced

150ml hot vegetable stock

1 tbsp chopped French parsley

20g dried cranberries

20g flaked almonds

20g pumpkin seeds

For the dressing

2 tbsp olive oil

1 tbsp apple cider vinegar

1 tbsp quality mayonnaise (shop-bought)

1 tsp Dijon mustard

METHOD

1. Preheat the oven to 190°c. Blend the grated onion with the sugar, salt, cayenne, black pepper and paprika in a food processor. Spread this mixture over the top and sides of the gammon joint.

2. Place the joint in a roasting tray and cover loosely with foil. Place the tray on the middle shelf of the preheated oven and cook for 1 hour 15 minutes, removing the foil for the last 30 minutes so the joint cooks uncovered. Check that the ham is piping hot throughout and the juices run clear before leaving it to stand for a few minutes.

3. While the ham is cooking, prepare the peach couscous. Place the couscous into a large bowl with the diced peach and pour over the hot vegetable stock. Cover the bowl with cling film and set aside for 4 to 5 minutes until the liquid has been absorbed.

4. Use a fork to fluff up the grains and lightly stir in the parsley, cranberries, almonds and pumpkin seeds. Whisk the olive oil and apple cider vinegar together, then drizzle this dressing over the couscous. Season to taste with salt and pepper.

5. In a small bowl, combine the mayonnaise with 1 teaspoon of water and the mustard. Carve the rested ham into slices and put some on serving plates (there will be leftovers).

6. Spoon the peach couscous onto the plates and serve the mustard mayonnaise on the side (I like to decant this into a small jug).

NOTES

Fluffing up the couscous makes the salad lighter. If the grains look a bit stiff after soaking, you can add a knob of butter or a little vegetable oil to break them up.

ROASTED PEACHES WITH AMARETTI & MASCARPONE

I love sinking my teeth into a juicy fresh peach, but they're also just heavenly when roasted. For this dish, choose peaches that are one day from fully ripe. The sweet, soft flesh pairs perfectly with warm spices and tart, creamy cheeses like mascarpone. Another perennial favourite in my kitchen.

Preparation time: 5 minutes | Cooking time: 20-25 minutes | Serves 2

INGREDIENTS

10 amaretti biscuits (I like the Vicenzi brand)

125ml mascarpone

1 tsp vanilla essence

100g golden caster sugar

25g unsalted butter, cubed

1 stick of cinnamon

1 star anise

3 large peaches

1 tsp amaretto (I like the Disaronno brand)

METHOD

1. Preheat the oven to 180°c. Break the amaretti biscuits into a small bowl. Mix the mascarpone and vanilla essence together in another bowl and set both bowls aside.

2. Sprinkle the sugar onto a non-stick baking tray and dot the cubes of butter around the tray. Break the cinnamon stick in half and add the pieces to the tray with the star anise.

3. Halve and destone the peaches, then place them cut-side down on top of the sugar, butter and spices. Roast in the preheated oven for 15 to 20 minutes, or until the peaches are soft but still holding their shape.

4. Remove the baking tray from the oven. Using a flat spatula, transfer the peaches to a warming plate and return them to the oven with the heat off and the door slightly ajar.

5. Discard the cinnamon and star anise, then scrape the caramelised sugar from the baking tray into a small saucepan over a medium heat and add the amaretto. Heat the mixture for just 1 or 2 minutes, to the consistency of runny honey.

6. Place 3 peach halves on each serving plate, add a generous dollop of the vanilla mascarpone, drizzle over the amaretto syrup and sprinkle with the amaretti biscuits.

NOTES

Some people like to discard the peach skins, rather than leaving them on. If you want to peel the peaches, use a small paring knife to make a cut at the top or bottom and pull back the skin gently.

If preferred, you can omit the star anise in the roasting process and replace the amaretto with liquorice sambuca, which has similar flavour notes.

CONDIMENTS

Condiments are the unsung heroes of the culinary world. Go into the food and drink section of any good bookshop and you will find lots of books on herbs and spices, but almost certainly none on condiments. Yet they grace nearly every kitchen in the world and while they grab less attention, they punch above their weight, adding concentrated shots of flavour and an extra layer of yumminess.

Condiments represent the second set of Go-With Foods that you need to include in your magical kitchen. They cover salts, oils, vinegars, mustards, bottled sauces, pastes and preserves. Unlike scents, where you pair with foods such as pork and beans, condiments link to specific cuisines: pesto in Mediterranean dishes, plum sauce in Chinese cooking and pomegranate molasses in Middle Eastern meals.

The joy of condiments is the nuances they bring to cooking. If you wanted to make a bright and acidic dressing for a simple lettuce salad, a good choice would be something like safflower oil with apple cider vinegar and a touch of lime juice. If you wanted a dressing for a more complex Asian salad, you could go in a completely different direction with ingredients like rice vinegar, soy sauce and white miso.

I think condiments are undervalued for a few reasons. Almost every condiment comes in a tin, can or jar and is mostly hidden away in cupboards and pantries. Their labels are good at giving us lists of ingredients, but less good at suggesting what to do with the condiment in question. For fear of embarrassing ourselves, I suspect we also avoid condiments that we can't pronounce, like Korean gochujang, which I did have to look up on the internet (koh-choo-jan(g)) when it first turned up in my local supermarket.

Despite these limitations, I have enormous faith in condiments. They are not expensive and they have long shelf lives. As long as you buy authentic versions where possible, you really cannot go wrong when working them into recipes old and new, based on your favourite foods.

Getting to grips with condiments

✦ Condiment Families

✦ Condiment Clusters

✦ Using Condiments in Cooking

Becoming confident with condiments will be an absolute doddle if you draw on what I call **Condiment Families**. Inside my pantry cupboard I have a printed list of condiments that I look at from time to time, largely to remind me what I might be missing and need to buy. Compared to my Scent Capsules, my collection of condiments is at least three times bigger. Samin Nosrat vividly highlighted the importance of condiments in her simply amazing book, *Salt, Fat, Acid, Heat*, bringing them out of the shadows and impressing upon us the need to celebrate these foodstuffs. In no particular order, these are key condiments you want to stock:

Salts

Having been convinced by professional chefs and cooks that different salts have different properties and are better (or worse) for different dishes, I would recommend you have at least two salts in your kitchen. If you only want one, I suggest you choose between sea salt and kosher salt.

- Table Salt – small, dense, cube-shaped, and very salty.
- Sea Salt – natural, flake-shaped, and goes by the names fleur de sel, sel gris and Maldon. Don't use these for cooking pasta, as the standout feature of sea salts is their texture, which gets lost once tossed into boiling water.
- Kosher Salt – good value for money and great for everyday cooking.

Oils

Choosing oils is all about the 'smoke point' and the fats (good, saturated). You don't need the whole suite of oils, but if you are really into cooking, I suggest you buy smaller bottles to save your pocket.

✦ Avocado Oil – a 'good fat' with a high smoke point (500+ degrees). Used for sautéing, roasting, searing and vinaigrettes alike. Prefers cool cupboards to fridges.

✦ Toasted Nut Oils (walnut, hazelnut, pistachio) – low smoke point. Big on flavour, great for vinaigrettes. Turns up in baking as an alternative to other fats.

✦ Sesame Oil – high smoke point. Used for sautés, roasts, and more. A must-have for Asian cuisines.

✦ Coconut Oil – solid at room temperature, high in saturated fats, widely used in South East Asia and India.

✦ Groundnut/Peanut/Canola/Rapeseed/Grapeseed/Vegetable Oil – interchangeable, middling to high smoke points. Good for deep-frying and stir-frying. Groundnut and peanut are best for Asian salads and stir-fries. Grapeseed is good for salad dressings.

✦ Sunflower/Safflower Oil – all-purpose oils, versatile, often used when making mayonnaise.

✦ Olive oil – rich in monounsaturated fat, best for Mediterranean dishes.

Vinegars

Vinegars are all about taste and some are quite expensive. I suggest you take a long, cool look at which of these you want to stock in your kitchen, which include:

✦ Red and White Vinegars – all-rounders in European cooking, used in dressings and mayonnaises. Also good for deglazing pans when roasting, frying and making casseroles.

✦ Balsamic Vinegar – hugely popular. Rich, dark, mellow, with a concentrated flavour. Turns up in oodles of dressings and with strawberries.

✦ Sherry Vinegar – sweeter than balsamic, but otherwise similar. Shows up more often in Iberian dishes than Italian ones.

✦ Apple Cider Vinegar – sharper than white vinegar. Can be used to pickle fruits such as pears.

✦ Rice Vinegar – comes in three versions (red and black in China, brown in Japan). Central to sweet and sour, and hot and sour dishes in Chinese and Thai cuisines.

✦ Flavoured Vinegars – often expensive. Any vinegar that goes by the name 'Lemon, Basil, Bay and Juniper' must surely be in danger of being confused with a Jo Malone perfume. If you must use them, make your own. Buy a litre of your preferred vinegar, fill up any old empty bottle with a working screw top and toss in whatever takes your fancy: raspberries, tarragon, fennel seeds…

Mustards

Commonly paired with meat and cheese, turns up in sandwiches, hot dogs and hamburgers. The major five varieties of mustard are English, American, French, German and wholegrain.

Preserves

Almost all preserves are fruit or vegetable-based, and they burst with sweet and sour tastes. Key preserves include piccalilli, chutney, sundried tomatoes, capers, gherkins, lemons, kimchi and sauerkraut.

Sauces and pastes

There are hundreds of bottled sauces and pastes available to you, spanning many national cuisines. Nowadays, supermarkets carry a vast range of these foodstuffs and should you shop at a specialist, you would find even more of them, reflecting sub-regional cuisines. I can't begin to list all the sauces and pastes that you might want to engage with, but here is my 'primer' for those of you who want to try new cuisines and dishes, alongside your current favourites.

- ✦ **Western** – ketchup, mayonnaise, Worcestershire sauce, HP sauce, mint sauce, horseradish, cranberry sauce, Cumberland sauce, pesto, tapenade, salad cream, barbecue sauce, Tabasco, salsa, guacamole, maple syrup, honey.
- ✦ **Eastern** – tahini, harissa, pomegranate molasses, date syrup, rosewater and orange blossom water, red pepper paste, plum sauce, hoisin sauce, XO sauce, oyster sauce, fish and shrimp sauce, soy sauce, bean paste, peanut paste, dashi, mirin, ponzu, wasabi, gochujang, sambal, sriracha.

With so many condiments available to us now, keeping them in check requires a bit of sorting. In the same way I came up with the idea of creating Scent Capsules for managing my herbs and spices, I came up with a similar idea for **Condiment Clusters** to manage all my bottles, jars, cans and packets. These are simply groups of kindred condiments, which I store in a mixture of containers in my pantry: narrow and high for oils and vinegars, wide and shallow for mustards, sauces, pastes and preserves. Having tested different ways to manage them over the years, I realised there were some cuisines that I loved, for which I had many recipes to choose from that I cooked regularly. For other cuisines, I had just a few recipes that were firm favourites. Reflecting on this, I came up with three Condiment Clusters:

✦ The cuisines I made most would require **All-Out Clusters**. These would have a large range of condiments, because I was working with them all the time.

✦ The cuisines I made regularly, but not weekly, would need some **Small-Scale Clusters**. These would have a smaller range of condiments aligned to those dishes, just enough to be authentic.

✦ Specific dishes and cuisines I made on special occasions would require a few **One-Off Clusters**. These would be for condiments that had long shelf-lives, which I could draw on as and when I needed.

There is a temptation to buy every type of condiment you can lay your hands on but, in truth, you can create a slimmed-down supply, simply by rotating your cuisines and dishes appropriately. Instead of working through a dozen different cuisines in a month, choose maybe half of those. That way you use those condiments more often, in less time, which helps you manage the risk of leaving jars and bottles half-used.

How many clusters you keep in your magical kitchen is up to you. Normally, I have two large containers for my All-Out Clusters, two medium containers for Small-Scale Clusters and a small container for One-Off Clusters, all in the same pantry. A few condiments go into the fridge once opened, like salsas and tapenades. Sometimes I add a new Small-Scale Cluster (typically when I have come back from a holiday) and sometimes I let one go. Sometimes it comes back, sometimes it doesn't, but you can see how flexible they are when these collections of condiments work for you.

So, where in your kitchen do you store your condiments right now? Are they in the pantry, strewn about in cupboards, or in your fridge? Alternatively, as once I had to do, have you tucked them underneath the bed in the spare room or stacked them in the closet? If you are finding it hard to make the best of your kitchen space, clusters may be a way of consolidating your magical kitchen.

The link between condiments and cuisines makes it much easier to work out how to use condiments in cooking. The larger the range of cuisines you want to cook (or want to learn to cook), the greater the number of condiments you will need, and the larger the financial investment you will have to make. **Using condiments in cooking** is reasonably straightforward. Quality recipes will give you the best ratios to use them in and, equally importantly, they should state early in the recipe whether the condiments are added during or after cooking. As a general rule:

✦   Salts, oils and vinegars are added during cooking.

✦   Mustard can be added during or after cooking.

✦   Most Eastern-based sauces and pastes are added during cooking.

✦   Most Western-based sauces are added after cooking.

✦   Preserves are made weeks or months before cooking and added after cooking.

✦   Salad dressings (which can include salts, oils, vinegars, mustards and sugars) are best made on the day and added to the salad once made.

It is up to you how tight or loose you want your condiment clusters to be. Foodies might go for specific locales or countries, such as Mexican or Thai. If you are hooked on a particular cuisine or have inherited a cuisine or two through your family, then very likely that will be the largest cluster you create. What you need to avoid at all costs, however, is having a shedload of just-in-case condiments. In my experience, two or three clusters will definitely get you by, but four or five is probably what you should aim for in order to make the most of your Go-To and Magical Foods. What matters most is that you have at least five recipes or dishes that draw on each of your clusters, to make buying condiments economical.

My journey with condiments

I can't tell you how many trials it took to get the right condiments in my kitchen, but once the cluster system fell into place, even the Resident Husband could find all those unsung heroes in a flash. My first All-Out Cluster included condiments native to west Mediterranean cuisines. These use common condiments like red and wine vinegars, nut- and olive-based oils, mustards, tomato purée, pesto, pistou and tapenades. These took up a whole shelf in my pantry: two high and narrow containers for the bottles, and a short and wide one for the jars and packets. The one drawback in my grand plan was where to keep added-after-cooking condiments like ketchup, HP and barbecue sauce. I don't use these often, but you can't not have them around for weekend brunches!

My first Small-Scale Cluster related to one of my favourite cuisines: Japanese. My first taste of Japanese food was on a holiday in Hawaii. To this day, I occasionally pop into a Benihana restaurant, mostly for the food but also the theatrics, with chefs wielding knives with aplomb! Japanese cuisine is challenging to cook, but I am a sucker for salty and umami tastes so I just had to make sure I always had soy sauce, mirin, rice vinegar, miso, tonkatsu sauce, nori (seaweed) and dashi broth in my kitchen.

My One-Off Cluster drew on the condiments required for Moroccan tagines and mezzes requiring chermoula, honey, tahini, preserved lemons, harissa paste, pomegranate molasses, date syrups and rose and orange blossom waters. All of these condiments have a very long shelf-life, which means all I have to do when I want to cook these dishes on special occasions is buy a few of my Magical Foods, like chicken, lamb and couscous.'

My **Stardust Tip** for condiments is to buy imported products for Asian, Middle Eastern and Southern American sauces and pastes. Search out high-quality suppliers for some of the more exotic ones. They will be more expensive, but they will be more authentic. Bear in mind these products have a long shelf-life, so it's worth the investment. Salts, oils, vinegars and mustards are worth buying at a mid-price or above, especially when you're adding them after cooking, when you want the taste and flavours to be fresh. Regular sauces and pastes like ketchup and mayonnaise are easy to find. Supermarkets do a great job of sourcing new products, but some exporters may adjust or dilute the ingredients to cater to the mainstream. Lastly, keep an eye on any E numbers in the list of ingredients: those above 400 get you into the less healthy category of additives like thickeners and stabilisers, which you really don't want to eat.

Take a look at the next recipes for using condiments in cooking.

Once you understand the foundations of cooking – whatever kind you like, whether it's French or Italian or Japanese – you really don't need a cookbook anymore.

Thomas Keller

BREADCRUMBED GOAT'S CHEESE

Rounds of creamy goat's cheese are coated in breadcrumbs and ground almonds then deep-fried for this recipe. I serve them with an elegant salad full of zesty vinegars, nutty oils and contrasting textures to cut through the richness of the cheese.

Preparation time: 20 minutes | Cooking time: 10 minutes | Serves 2

INGREDIENTS

2 rounds of goat's cheese

2 tbsp plain flour

1 egg

100g breadcrumbs

25g ground almonds

Salt and pepper

300ml sunflower oil

For the salad and dressing

60g mixed hardy salad leaves (such as baby red oak, romaine or frisée lettuce)

1 shallot, finely chopped

1 tsp chopped fresh chives

30ml sherry vinegar

60ml groundnut oil

60ml hazelnut oil

2 tbsp chopped hazelnuts

Salt and pepper

METHOD

1. Preheat the oven to 60°c. Lay out three plates on your kitchen bench, tip the flour onto the first plate, crack the egg onto the second and beat with a small whisk or fork.

2. Mix the breadcrumbs, ground almonds and some salt and pepper in a small bowl, then tip the mix onto the third plate.

3. Coat the cheeses in the flour and dust off any of the excess. Dip them into the beaten egg, then roll them in the breadcrumb mixture, pressing firmly so the coating sticks. Transfer to a plate and leave in the fridge on a lower shelf.

4. For the salad, combine the leaves, chopped shallot and chives in a serving bowl. Keep in the fridge until ready to serve. For the dressing, combine the vinegar with the oils then stir in the chopped hazelnuts. Season with salt and pepper to taste.

5. Fill a large saucepan over a high heat with the sunflower oil and let it reach 170°c. Lower the chilled and coated cheeses into the hot oil with a slotted spoon and deep-fry for 2 to 3 minutes until golden brown. Transfer them to a plate lined with kitchen paper to drain off the oil, then place on a baking tray and cook in the preheated oven for 3 minutes.

6. Remove the cheeses from the oven and transfer to serving plates. Divide the salad between them and drizzle over the dressing.

NOTES

Sometimes the beaten egg doesn't completely coat the cheese, leaving a few bare patches. If that happens, gently spread the egg out with your fingers.

For the salad, it's important to dry the leaves thoroughly after washing them, because you simply will not taste the dressing if they are wet.

BIBIMBAP

If you have never heard of this Korean street food, you are in for a treat. Bibimbap literally means mixed rice, which sounds simple, but this isn't the easiest dish to bring together so you might need to make it a few times before you can get it just right.

Preparation time: 30 minutes, plus 30 minutes marinating (optional) | Cooking time: 35 minutes | Serves 2

INGREDIENTS

200g white or brown rice

50g courgette, sliced

50g carrot, cut into batons

50g chestnut mushrooms

25g baby spinach leaves

1 tbsp + 2 tsp vegetable oil

2 large fresh eggs

For the beef (optional)

100g lean beef strips

3 cloves of garlic, finely chopped

1 tbsp soy sauce

1 tbsp maple syrup

2 tsp sesame oil

For the sauce

1½ tsp soy sauce

2 tbsp mirin

2 tbsp rice vinegar

4 tbsp gochujang paste (I use the Sous Chef brand)

3 tsp golden caster sugar

2½ tsp sesame oil

1 clove of garlic, finely chopped

METHOD

1. Preheat the oven to 60°c. If you are adding beef, place the strips into a shallow tray or bowl and add the garlic, soy sauce, maple syrup and sesame oil. Leave to marinate for 30 minutes.

2. For the sauce, whisk the soy sauce, mirin and rice vinegar into the gochujang paste. Stir in the sugar, sesame oil and garlic. Set aside.

3. Add the rice to a saucepan, cover with water and bring to the boil. Put the lid on tightly, turn the heat down and simmer for 15 to 20 minutes. Turn off the heat and leave the rice in the pan with the lid on while you prepare the other ingredients.

4. If using, place the marinated beef strips into a non-stick frying pan and cook for 3 to 4 minutes over a high heat until lightly caramelised. Transfer to a plate and place in the oven.

5. Add 1 teaspoon of the vegetable oil to a separate non-stick frying pan over a medium-high heat. Place the courgettes and carrots on the opposite sides of the pan and cook for 4 minutes, then transfer them to the oven.

6. Add another teaspoon of vegetable oil to the pan and cook the mushrooms in the same way for 2 minutes. Pop them in the oven, cook the baby spinach for 1 minute then remove it from the pan.

7. In a clean pan, heat the remaining tablespoon of vegetable oil over a high heat. Crack the eggs one at a time into the centre and cook until done to your liking.

8. Quickly divide the rice between two deep bowls. Add all the vegetables (and beef, if using) then pour the sauce around the perimeter and place the eggs on top.

NOTES

What makes this dish is the gochujang, a Korean fermented red pepper paste that is sweet, spicy and slightly funky (in a good way!) which can be found online or in Asian supermarkets. Do try it!

CALIFORNIAN LAMB FAJITAS

I ate my first fajitas in downtown Los Angeles when Californian cuisine was all the rage in the 90s. I've tweaked a version of that dish using lamb steaks, complemented by cooling sour cream, bright guacamole and soft tortillas, with a few Asian notes from the hoisin and soy sauce marinade.

Preparation time: 15-20 minutes | Cooking time: 15 minutes | Serves 2

INGREDIENTS

6 flour tortillas

2 x 300g lamb rump steaks

1 tbsp hoisin sauce

2 tsp dark soy sauce

2 tsp + 2 tbsp safflower oil

1 red pepper

4 spring onions

4 cloves of garlic

1 tbsp cornflour, mixed with 1 tbsp water

1 small jar of your favourite salsa dip (I like Dorito's Hot Salsa)

300ml sour cream

For the guacamole

2 ripe avocados

2 limes, juiced

1 red chilli, finely diced (optional)

½ small red onion, finely diced

Small handful of fresh coriander, chopped

Splash of extra virgin olive oil (optional)

For the sauce

1 tbsp dry sherry

1 tbsp dark soy sauce

2 tsp Spanish sherry vinegar

1 tsp sweet chilli sauce

½ tsp brown sugar

¼ tsp salt

METHOD

1. Preheat the oven to 170°c and wrap the stack of flour tortillas in tin foil, ready for warming in the oven later.

2. Use a very sharp knife to cut the lamb steaks across the grain into 1cm strips. Place them in a large bowl, then stir in the hoisin and soy sauces with 2 teaspoons of the safflower oil to marinate.

3. Top and tail the red pepper, remove the white innards and seeds, then cut into thin strips. Slice the spring onions into 2cm pieces on the diagonal. Finely chop the garlic, then put the prepared ingredients into a small bowl.

4. For the guacamole, halve the avocados, remove the stones, scoop out the flesh and mash with a fork. Combine this with the remaining ingredients, cover and place in the fridge.

5. For the sauce, simply combine all the ingredients in a small bowl. At this stage, place the foil-wrapped tortillas in the preheated oven to heat for 10 minutes.

6. Meanwhile, place a wok over a high heat. When hot, add the remaining 2 tablespoons of safflower oil and tilt the wok to coat the base and sides. Stir-fry the marinated strips of lamb for 1 minute, then add the pepper, spring onion and garlic to the wok.

7. Pour the prepared sauce into the wok. When it comes to a low boil, stir in the cornflour mixture so that it glazes the lamb. This should take 2 to 4 minutes altogether. Taste and adjust the seasoning as needed.

8. Spoon the fajita mixture onto a heated platter and serve it with the salsa, guacamole, sour cream and hot flour tortillas.

NIKKEI SEA BASS

Fusion food combines elements of culinary traditions that originate from different countries, regions and cultures. Nikkei cuisine is a love match between Japanese and Peruvian food and techniques, like curing fish. Sea bass is super healthy and tasty when prepared this way.

Preparation time: 2 hours 30 minutes | Serves 2

INGREDIENTS

2 pin-boned sea bass fillets

For the leche de tigre

75ml white fish stock

60ml lime juice

60ml lemon juice

50g fresh cod, chopped

1 stick of celery, chopped

1 clove of garlic, crushed

1 tsp grated fresh ginger

$\frac{1}{2}$ tsp instant dashi powder

$\frac{1}{2}$ tsp salt

1 mini orange sweet pepper

For the garnish

1 small red onion

4 small Persian cucumbers

1 tbsp roughly chopped fresh coriander

$\frac{1}{2}$-1 tsp shichimi togarashi

METHOD

1. For the leche de tigre, put all the ingredients except the orange pepper into a blender and blitz until the mixture is white, frothy and smooth (around 30 to 60 seconds). Finely chop the orange pepper, add this to the blender and blitz for a further 30 seconds. Leave to rest for 15 minutes.

2. Pour the leche de tigre through a sieve into an airtight container and discard any solids. Store in the fridge for at least 2 hours.

3. When the leche de tigre is ready, slice the red onion into rings and dice the cucumbers. Place the sea bass fillets on a long platter, spoon the leche de tigre over and around the sea bass, then leave it to cure for 5 minutes.

4. Finally, scatter the onion and cucumber on top of the fillets and sprinkle the fresh coriander on top. Dust with the shichimi togarashi and serve.

NOTES

To add some crunch to this dish, you could serve the sea bass with Swedish crispbreads or similar accompaniments. A tart Scandinavian salad would also go well with the fish; simply combine a generous helping of peppery watercress, chopped shallots and fresh dill with a lemon and white vinegar dressing.

PERSIAN BAKLAVA

I got into these sweet treats in Australia, where there are large communities of people from southern-eastern European countries, where baklava comes from. This is a slightly time-consuming dish, but it is really worth the effort. There's nothing better than homemade baklava and it's always a crowd favourite.

Preparation time: 1 hour, plus 1 hour resting | Cooking time: 50-55 minutes | Serves 4 or more

INGREDIENTS

270g ready-made filo pastry (I use the Jus-Rol brand)

125g pure butter ghee

60g almonds

60g walnuts

60g hazelnuts

1 tsp sugar

1 tsp rosewater

Flour, for dusting

For the syrup

50ml water

50ml honey

40g golden caster sugar

$\frac{1}{4}$ tsp ground cardamom

$\frac{1}{4}$ tsp ground cinnamon

1 lemon, juiced

METHOD

1. If the filo pastry is frozen, transfer it to the fridge 24 hours before you want to use it. If you have bought fresh filo, you can start to work with it immediately.

2. For the syrup, combine all the ingredients in a saucepan over a low-medium heat. Bring to the boil and let it simmer for 10 minutes, then remove from the heat and leave to cool.

3. Meanwhile, preheat the oven to 200°c and brush a baking tray with some of the ghee. Chop all the nuts into evenly sized pieces and mix them with the sugar and rosewater. Set aside.

4. Flour your kitchen bench and begin by laying down the first sheet of filo pastry. Brush the entire sheet with ghee, then lay the next one on top and repeat so that you have 3 sheets of filo coated in ghee in a stack. Keep the remaining pastry sheets under a damp towel to stop them drying out.

5. Spoon half of the nut mixture onto the shorter end of the filo stack in a horizontal line, leaving a 1cm border along the bottom edge of the pastry.

6. Roll up the baklava by pulling up the end of the stack and tucking it over the filling as tightly as possible. Continue rolling until you almost reach the end of the pastry, then use an extra dab of ghee to seal the edges.

7. Slice the baklava roll into 5cm pieces and place these on the baking tray with no spaces in between. Repeat steps 4 to 7 (you may have a sheet of pastry left over).

8. Bake the baklava in the preheated oven for 35 to 40 minutes until golden brown. Remove it from the oven and pour over the cooled syrup immediately.

9. Let the baklava rest for about 1 hour in the baking tray. This will allow all the syrup to soak into the pastry.

10. Once rested, use a metal spatula to transfer the baklava to a serving board and cut into squares or slices.

POTIONS

Potions are the last set of Co-With Foods. Most world cuisines have a long tradition of pairing food with alcohol. Properly used, it adds instant oomph to savoury and sweet dishes and is a great way to transform foods. All you need to know is how to unlock its magic. Which boozy Potions you want to keep in your kitchen will be influenced by your appetite for alcohol, what tastes and flavours you like most, and whether you make more savoury dishes than sweet ones.

Alcohol is a versatile pick-me-up in cooking. Most (but not all) alcohol will burn off during cooking and most recipes don't even use all that much compared to the serving size of a glass of wine. When you open a bottle of wine or whisky, you can smell the underlying ingredients right away because the alcohol molecules are volatile, meaning they evaporate rapidly into the air. That's why we add a splash of kirsch to a fruit salad; it helps to convey the aromas to our nostrils, enhancing our overall enjoyment of the dish. You can't get drunk from a boozy dish but you will certainly get a kick from it, in the nicest sense!

Favourite savoury dishes of mine include falling-off-the-bone short ribs braised in dry red wine, Riesling chicken where the white wine marries with bacon and mushrooms in a sinfully creamy sauce, leek risotto with champagne and grilled prawns, pulled pork elevated by a honey bourbon sauce, and the perennial penne alla vodka. I also love to use potions in sweet dishes like my gin and tonic cheesecake, blood orange crème brûlée with champagne (quite a lot of champers turns up in my meals) and baked peaches with amaretto syrup.

Water-based foods like meat, fish and fruit absorb alcohol molecules into their cells. When you poach, stew or marinate these foods, you extract more of their underlying tastes and flavours. Adding even a tablespoon of vodka to a savoury or sweet dish will do the trick. From golden autumns and icy winters to cool springs and summer heatwaves, you can find any number of malty beers, sweet ciders, fruity wines, kick-ass spirits and sublime liqueurs to align with your favourite dishes throughout the year, adding elegance and complexity all the way from absinthe to whisky.

Getting to grips with potions

✦ Alcohol Strength

✦ Alcohol Properties

✦ Using Alcohol in Cooking

Winemakers and brewers measure **Alcohol Strength** in two ways: alcohol content by volume (ABV) and proof, which is approximately twice the ABV. Therefore, a vodka that is 40% ABV is 80 proof. The higher the proof, the more intoxicating the drink. In cooking, the higher the ABV, the more intense the flavours will be. Moreover, the shorter the cooking time, the more alcohol will be retained.

If you add alcohol to boiling liquid and remove it instantly from the heat, up to about 85% will be retained. If you add alcohol to cold liquid (juice for example), the retention falls to about 70%. If baking or simmering, the longer it goes on (from 15 minutes to a couple of hours), the less alcohol is retained: anything from around 45% to as low as 10%.

So that you don't have to look up all the ABVs for alcohol, here is a primer on the most-used potions used in cooking:

✦ **Beers** swing wildly from low-alcohol lagers to teeth-numbing IPAs and stouts, from 3% to 9% ABV.

✦ **Wines** range from 5% to 20%. Most white wines hover between 7% and 13%, while reds loiter between 12% and 15%. Dessert wines are at the upper end, between 17% and 21%, as are heavier fortified wines like Ports, sherries and Madeira. French and Italian vermouths also fall within this range.

✦ **Spirits** start from 35% to 40% for brandy and cognac, a standard 40% for gin and vodka, and between 40% to 65% for whisky and bourbon. The standard for tequila and rum is 40%, but rum is often over-proofed to 75%. Now you know why those boozy rum cakes are so appealing!

✦ **Liqueurs** are basically sweetened and diluted forms of wines and spirits. Typically, liqueurs range from 15% to 55% ABV.

Alcohol Properties of potions are all food-based: grains, fruits, potatoes, sugars, herbs and spices. When introducing alcohol to foods, you need to align the underlying ingredients of the booze with the flavours of the foods, based on the principles of flavour pairings you read about earlier. Take tiramisu, for example. Coffee-soaked sponge fingers and mildly sweet mascarpone simply scream for an almond or hazelnut-based potion, like Disaronno and Frangelico. You could also use a coffee-based potion, like Kahlua, for harmony (personally I find this combination too samey same, but I know others love this pairing). In the savoury realm, apple-based Calvados is a must-have for Chicken Normandy and Roast Pork Loin withApples.

On the opposite page you can see a list of some of the most popular potions used in cooking and the flavours they produce, like coconut-based Malibu, which would go well with pineapple, cherry, chocolate and lime. Just so you know what an awful pairing might be, imagine a mild fillet of cod with a Port-based sauce; the delicate fish would clash terribly with the sweet flavours of raspberry, blackberry and chocolate in the alcohol. Nor would you want to pair a light and zingy lemon posset with a few tablespoons of over-proofed dark rum, which would overwhelm the dish.

Shortcuts
Classic Potions

Fortified wines

Madeira
Madeiran – Brandy

Marsala
Sicilian – Brandy

Moscatel
Portuguese – Grape

Port
Portuguese – Grape

Sherry
Spanish – Grape

Vermouth
Italian – Diverse herbs and spices

Fruit & grain wines

Reds and Whites
Australasian, American, European – Grapes

Beers
Australasian, American, European, Asian – Grains, Hops

Mirin
Japan – Rice

Sake
Japan – Rice

Liqueurs

Advocaat
Dutch – Orange/Lemon/ Cherry/Vanilla

Amaretto
Italian – Almond

Cointreau
French – Bitter Orange

Crème de Cassis
French – Blackcurrant

Crème de Framboise
French – Strawberry

Curacao
Dutch – Bitter Orange (aka triple sec)

Disaronno
Italian – Almond (aka amaretto)

Drambuie
Scottish – Whisky/Honey/ Heather/Herbs

Frangelico
Italian – Hazelnut

Goldwasser
Polish – Aniseed, Caraway seed/Citrus

Grand Marnier
French – Orange

Kahlua
Mexican – Coffee

Malibu
Caribbean – Coconut

Maraschino
Italian – Cherries

Pernod/Ricard
French – Liquorice/Aniseed

Poire William
Swiss – Pears

Sambuca
Italian – Elderberries/Aniseed

Tia Maria
Jamaican – Coffee/Spices

Spirits

Armagnac
French Brandy – Biscuit-y

Calvados
French Brandy – Apples

Gin
European – Junipers

Kirsch
German – Cherry

Mescal
Mexican – Agave

Rum
Caribbean – Sugars

Slivovitz
Bosnian-Serbian – Black Plum

Vodka
Russian/Polish – Potatoes

Whisky
Scottish – Grains

It's worth knowing the properties of fortified and dessert wines, spirits and liqueurs. Broadly speaking:

✦ **Fortified Wines** are grape-based wines to which the winemaker adds a distilled spirit, like brandy. These wines run the gamut from dry and fine to rich and raisin-y, but from the driest sherry to the deepest Port, you know that you are drinking something wine-based. Of the six fortified wines, shown on page 121, sherry and vermouth are the least heavy.

✦ **Spirits** are distilled by means of fermenting grain, fruit or vegetables. Juniper berries for gin; wine for brandy; sugars (including molasses and honey) for rum; blue agave plants for tequila; various grains (barley, corn, maize, rye, wheat) for whisky; and potatoes for vodka.

✦ **Liqueurs** are made from a distilled spirit and flavoured with fruit, herbs, spices, flowers, nuts or cream, then bottled with added sugars and sweeteners. Except for the fact that they are all intoxicating, the combination of aromas and tastes is what gives you a feel for the underlying ingredients, like berries, citrus fruits and nuts.

Using alcohol in cooking is relatively easy, but the number of ways you can cook with it may well surprise you. For sure, beers, ciders and wines have always been used in one-pot stews and casseroles for flavouring and deglazing, while adding a tipple (often brandy, rum or whisky) to cakes, puddings and trifles is nothing less than a national pastime. However, there are other methods that you might want to experiment with, some easier than others:

✦ Adding fortified wines, spirits and liqueurs to a fruity sauce which you brush over meat during cooking is called glazing. The glaze locks in moisture, helps the meat to cook through without drying out and adds a caramelised finish. Barbecue sauces with a touch of bourbon are great for chicken, as are fruity sauces with a dash of tequila. Pork glazed with an apple brandy sauce also works well.

✦ Showing off in your kitchen doesn't get much better than flambéing. You will need a high ABV potion to get this right. Pernod added to prawns while shallow frying is a classic combination. Dessert flambés typically begin with a few tablespoons of sugar in a shallow pan. Once the sugar turns amber gold, you add a few splashes of a darker spirit, like brandy or rum, ignite the alcohol and let it burn off, then pour the resulting sauce over your chosen fruit.

✦ Try adding wines and spirits to melted butter with complementary herbs, nuts and cheeses, which you pop into the freezer ahead of serving. These are great for toasts. Good choices for special occasions include crab butter with a splash of brandy and foie gras butter flavoured with Armagnac to pour over steak cuts, like sirloin.

✦ Softening whole or sliced fruit by soaking it in alcohol is called macerating, which turns into what some people call tipsy fruit. Softer fruits, like berries, have a shorter shelf life than hardier fruits like apples, pears and figs. The best time to macerate is when the fruit is just past its peak. Popular tipsy fruit recipes include brandied preserved figs, and berries soaked in gin.

✦ Adding dessert wines, beers (especially stout), spirits and liqueurs to cakes, tray bakes, pastries, puddings and desserts. Boozy bakes cover a vast canvas from light Aperol Spritz blancmanges to heavier margarita cheesecakes and brandy snaps with Baileys cream or Caribbean rum black cake.

✦ Simmering spirits and liqueurs with other ingredients (such as stock or butter) softens their fiery, boozy punch. Classic combinations include steak Diane with brandy, shrimp pasta with vodka, and grilled pork with mango and rum sauce. Other well-known sauces include claret wine for salmon and tuna; Champagne sauce for poached white fish like sole, turbot or John Dory; white wine in thermidor sauce for lobster; and Grand Marnier in mandarin sauce for duck or crêpes.

My journey with potions

The first potions I engaged with seriously were mostly used for baking; rum and brandy regularly turned up in my puddings and cakes. I vividly remember making an Austrian rum coffee cake in my early teens, pricking the cooled cake with cocktail sticks before pouring the dark rum all over the cake to soak in. Other boozy dishes included chocolate Guinness cupcakes for Christmas, rum babas in the summer and red wine poached pears in the autumn.

In my twenties, I only stocked my kitchen with a small bottle each of Italian vermouth and French brandy. Later on, when I had bit more money, I added sweet wines for desserts. As my culinary repertoire expanded, so too did my potion preserve, and my booze budget! The way I got around this was replacing bottles of spirits and liqueurs with **pocket-sized miniatures**. Alcohol generally has a long shelf life – up to a year – which makes it relatively good value. Nowadays, most bottle shops have a large range of fortified wines, spirits and liqueurs. I have around ten to fifteen miniatures, largely because I love baking but also because just even a small splash of something often helps me build up more layers in my dishes.

Having worked with alcohol (a lot!), I've come to think its purpose is akin to the resounding last chorus of a song: soaring violins and the choir belting their way through the final refrain, like the Heart duo (Ann and Nancy Wilson) playing *Stairway to Heaven* live at the Kennedy Centre Honors.

My **Stardust Tip** for potions is to align your choices with the seasons. Potions are not especially seasonal, and people drink the same wines, spirits and liqueurs all year round. However, when used in cooking, potions take on a seasonal aspect, because they add depth to the underlying ingredient. Bold reds turn up in hearty casseroles and stews. Warm, sweet, golden liqueurs find their way into fruity desserts and creamy puddings. While a good dish will always appeal, the time of year makes a difference. Grilled pork with a dark rum sauce in autumn will feel much more right than the same dish served in spring, whereas a piña colada popsicle based on white rum is best served in summer.

And now for more irresistible recipes using wines, spirits and liqueurs!

I love the alchemy of cooking, the theatre of it. It's creating something.
Anthony Warlow

FRENCH ONION SOUP WITH AN ITALIAN TWIST

Everyone needs a great recipe for boozy French onion soup. The original version of this one is from Delia Smith, which can't be beaten from my perspective. Croutons are always great here, but sometimes I like to replace these with Italian parmigiana toasts to add some Mediterranean flair.

Preparation time: 10 minutes | Cooking time: 1 hour 30 minutes | Serves 2

INGREDIENTS

25g butter

1 tbsp olive oil

350g brown onions, thinly sliced

2 cloves of garlic, thinly sliced

½ tsp golden caster sugar

600ml good beef stock

150ml white wine

1 tbsp brandy

Salt and pepper

For the topping

1 ficelle (a type of French bread similar to a baguette but smaller and thinner)

2 tbsp olive oil

4 tbsp tinned chopped tomatoes (I use the Napolini brand)

4 tbsp grated mozzarella

Fresh basil, finely chopped (optional)

METHOD

1. Melt the butter with the oil in a large saucepan on a high heat. Add the onions, garlic and sugar. Cook for 5 to 6 minutes, turning the onions every couple of minutes until they start to caramelise.

2. Reduce the heat and leave the onions to carry on cooking very slowly for about 25 to 30 minutes, until you have a rich, nut-brown mix.

3. Pour in the stock, white wine and brandy. Turn up the heat and stir with a wooden spoon, scraping the base of the pan well. When the liquid starts to simmer, turn the heat down to the lowest setting and leave the soup to cook very gently, without a lid, for about 45 to 60 minutes.

4. Halfway through cooking the soup, preheat the oven to 200°c for the topping. 10 minutes later, cut the bread into 2.5cm diagonal slices. Place them into a bowl and drizzle over the olive oil. Turn the slices in the oil with your hands.

5. Place the slices on a solid baking tray 3cm apart. Put them in the preheated oven for 10 minutes, turning them over halfway through. Meanwhile, drain the tinned tomatoes.

6. Remove the baking tray from the oven and divide the tomatoes between the slices. Scatter the grated mozzarella over the tomatoes.

7. Bake for another 5 to 10 minutes until the mozzarella starts to char. Lower the heat to 160°c if the cheese is at risk of burning. Turn off the oven when the toasts are ready, but leave the baking tray on the lowest shelf and keep the door open.

8. Taste the soup to check the seasoning, adding salt and pepper if needed, and give it a good stir for 1 to 2 minutes.

9. Ladle the soup into bowls and float the tomato and mozzarella toasts on top. Scatter them with some fresh basil if you like, then serve straightaway.

NOTES

You may want to invest in a couple of French soup crocks to keep soups hot after serving.

QUICK COQ AU VIN

This fuss-free, modern take on the classic French recipe cooks in half the time and uses dry white wine instead of red to bring out the flavour of the chicken and mushrooms. Perfect for date night or just bringing a bit of luxury to a midweek meal.

Preparation time: 15 minutes | Cooking time: 45 minutes | Serves 2

INGREDIENTS

4 cloves of garlic

200g closed cup mushrooms, halved

1 large brown onion, quartered

1 fennel bulb, sliced (leaves and root removed)

100g cherry tomatoes

160g smoked bacon lardons or pancetta cubes

2 sprigs each of rosemary and thyme

2 fresh bay leaves

2 tbsp olive oil

Salt and pepper, to taste

50g butter, at room temperature

4 pieces (approx. 500g) free-range chicken with the skin on (I use thighs and drumsticks)

250ml dry white wine

METHOD

1. Place a 26cm roasting tin into a cold oven and preheat to 180°c fan. Leaving the skins on, smash the garlic cloves with the flat side of a knife and put them in a large bowl with the mushrooms, onion, fennel, cherry tomatoes and lardons.

2. Tie the rosemary, thyme and bay leaves tightly together with white string and add this to the bowl, then drizzle over the olive oil and toss to coat all the veg. Season generously with salt and pepper, then set aside.

3. Mash the butter in another bowl with more salt and pepper. Rub the butter all over the chicken pieces, then wash your hands after handling the raw meat.

4. When the oven is up to temperature, throw the veg mixture into the roasting tin, place the chicken on top and cook on the middle shelf of the oven for 25 minutes.

5. After this time, add the wine to the roasting tin. Give it a good shake and return to the oven for a further 20 minutes.

6. Check that the chicken is cooked by pushing a skewer into the thickest part of a thigh; if the juices run clear, it is cooked through and ready to serve.

NOTES

I like to serve this with crusty bread to mop up all those lovely juices from the tin.

You can add a tablespoon each of chopped fresh thyme and rosemary to the butter before rubbing it over the chicken if you like, to give the dish even more flavour and fragrance.

SAFFRON & CHILLI PRAWN RISOTTO

Wine adds a lot of pizzazz to most risottos, extracting more of the key ingredients' underlying tastes and flavours. In my experience, it's better to use fresh prawns rather than frozen ones and liquid stock rather than cubes here, though neither is essential for this beautiful yet substantial dish.

Preparation time: 30 minutes | Cooking time: 20 minutes | Serves 2

INGREDIENTS

12 fresh green (raw) whole king prawns

400ml fish stock (I use the Potts brand)

50ml olive oil

2 tbsp minced red onion

2 tsp minced garlic

2 red chillies, minced

2 fresh medium tomatoes, peeled, deseeded and diced

175g Arborio rice, rinsed

75ml dry white wine

2 tsp saffron threads

10 basil leaves, torn

40g unsalted butter

Salt and pepper

METHOD

1. Peel and devein the king prawns. Set aside under a damp paper towel. Meanwhile, heat the fish stock in a medium saucepan to a rolling boil, then reduce the heat to a simmer.

2. Add the olive oil to a wide, heavy-based pan and sweat the minced onion, garlic and chilli over a medium heat.

3. Stir in the diced tomatoes and then add the rice. Cook for a couple of minutes, stirring constantly. Pour in the wine and when it has been absorbed, stir in the saffron threads.

4. Start adding the simmering fish stock in batches of 100ml, stirring frequently. Allow the rice to absorb the stock before adding another batch and repeat until there's one batch left. Over the next 15 to 20 minutes, the risotto will become creamy but the grains should still be intact and separate, with a little bite.

5. About 3 minutes before the risotto is ready, add the raw prawns and basil with the last 100ml of stock, stirring constantly. Cook just until the prawns are translucent.

6. Lastly, stir in the butter and season with salt and pepper to taste. Serve immediately, perhaps complemented with a fresh green salad on the side.

NOTES

Peeling a tomato is best done by carefully lowering the whole tomato into boiling water. Remove it after 30 seconds, or when the skin begins to peel back, and transfer straight into iced water to cool.

If the saffron threads don't give the risotto a nice vibrant colour, you can add a teaspoon of turmeric towards the end of cooking.

BOURBON-GLAZED CHICKEN DRUMSTICKS WITH GREENS

Booze really does help mild meats like chicken. Bourbon is a type of American whiskey made with corn, and the high alcohol proof makes the glaze nice and sticky. These delicious drumsticks are a southern American favourite and can be served with any seasonal greens; I like purple sprouting broccoli.

Preparation time: 10 minutes | Cooking time: 35-40 minutes | Serves 2

INGREDIENTS

6-8 chicken drumsticks

2 spring onions

200g purple sprouting broccoli

For the bourbon glaze

1 tbsp vegetable oil

30g onion, minced

100ml ketchup

30g molasses

15g brown sugar

1 tbsp Worcestershire sauce

1 tbsp apple cider vinegar

2 tsp English yellow mustard powder (I like the Colman's brand)

1 tsp coarse salt

$\frac{1}{2}$ tsp black pepper

30ml bourbon

METHOD

1. Take the chicken drumsticks out of the fridge 30 minutes before you want to start cooking, so they come up to room temperature. Preheat the oven to 200°c.

2. Season the drumsticks with salt and pepper, then place them on a non-stick baking tray and cook in the preheated oven for 15 minutes.

3. While the drumsticks are cooking, make the bourbon glaze. Heat the vegetable oil in a large saucepan over a medium heat. Add the minced onion and sweat for a couple of minutes, then stir in all the remaining ingredients except the bourbon.

4. Reduce the heat to low-medium and simmer the sauce for 7 minutes, then add the bourbon to the pan and cook for another 3 minutes or so, until it thickens to a glaze. Turn the heat down to the lowest setting.

5. Remove the drumsticks from the oven and pour over half of the bourbon sauce. Return the drumsticks to the oven for another 20 to 25 minutes. If you have one, use a small meat thermometer to check the internal temperature of the chicken which should be around 75°c.

6. While the drumsticks are cooking, slice the spring onions on the diagonal and cook the broccoli in a large pan of boiling water for 3 to 5 minutes, until tender.

7. Keep the remaining glaze on a low heat, barely simmering. When the drumsticks are almost done, turn the heat up to medium and taste the glaze to check the seasoning.

8. Remove the drumsticks from the oven and use tongs to plate them. Add the broccoli and pour the reserved glaze over the chicken. Garnish with the sliced spring onions.

NOTES

Keep an eye on the timings for this dish, as you are cooking things simultaneously. I often work backwards from a planned serving time. If I intended to eat this dish at 7:30pm, I would need to start cooking at approximately 6:50pm. Parallel processes are one of the fundamentals of good cooking, so it is worth starting with recipes like this, where you can experiment with just a couple of elements.

PIÑA COLADA POPSICLES

This is one of my whimsical, boozy desserts for summer days, usually when the Resident Husband is doing a barbecue. You will need a set of ice lolly moulds and I recommend you buy the larger ones for us adults! You should get six popsicles from this recipe.

Preparation time: 15 minutes, plus 4 hours freezing | Serves 6

INGREDIENTS

300g fresh pineapple

150ml coconut cream, plus extra for dipping

50ml coconut milk

100ml white rum

2 tbsp fresh lime juice

2g ice cream stabiliser (optional)

15g coconut flakes

15g toasted flaked almonds

METHOD

1. If you are starting with a whole pineapple, remove the top and bottom, cut off the tough outer skin, quarter it, take out the core and weigh the remaining fruit. Chop 300g of the prepared pineapple into small chunks.

2. Give the coconut cream and milk tins a good shake before measuring out.

3. Put all the ingredients except the stabiliser, coconut flakes and toasted almonds into a food processor and blend until you have a smooth purée. If using, whisk in the stabiliser by hand.

4. Divide the piña colada mix evenly between the popsicle moulds and freeze until solid. This will take at least 4 hours.

5. When the popsicles are almost ready to serve, combine the coconut flakes and toasted almonds in a small bowl and pour the extra coconut cream into a small jug.

6. Unmould the frozen popsicles, then dip the tops into the jug of coconut cream to coat them and dip gently into the coconut-almond mix so it sticks. Serve immediately.

NOTES

Other popular boozy mixes you could try include peach bellini, watermelon vodka and mojito popsicles. My favourite is the piña colada mix though; I like this tropical version for the taste alone, but what makes it a hit for me is the creamy, luscious texture.

FINISHES

COLOURS

Day in, day out, billions of people reach for staple foods like barley, corn, couscous, millet, oats, potatoes, rice, rye and wheat-based products like bread, pasta and noodles. The majority of these are starchy carbohydrates and most of them are shades of beige.

Beige foods have taken a bit of a hit in the last few years, tainted by worries that many beige by-products – like sandwiches, chips and crisps – are largely unappetising and unhealthy. Without beige foods, however, the world would be in a desperate place. We need their essential nutrients for wellness and health, and beige grain-based foods have a much longer shelf life than other perishable sources of carbohydrate.

I like beige foods and their by-products. Beige foods are like comfort blankets. They help us out on those days when we get home from work late, when we are tired and have neither the time nor the energy to cook. They are also inexpensive. However, they do have a few cons. They are less visually appealing compared to sunny yellow citrus fruits, bright red tomatoes, green leafy vegetables and purple berries, and seriously lacking in texture. Beige foods don't deserve bashing though. Far worse are all those 'dead foods' that have virtually no nutritional value, bereft of minerals, vitamins and fibres after being packaged and preserved, like reconstituted guacamole, frozen fish sticks and sandwich fillers.

Including fresh, colourful foods in our meals benefits us home cooks in two ways. First, they deliver essential nutrients to our bodies, keeping us healthy. Second, they pretty up our dishes! Given the amazing range of colours in nature, the best way to get inspired in our kitchens is to make room for as many rainbow foods as we can, with a little help from our favourite beige foods.

Getting to grips with colours

✦ Colourful Riots

✦ Nutritious Colours

✦ Using Colours in Cooking

There is no obstacle to you creating **Colourful Riots** in your kitchen. You simply need to brush up on the principles for using colours, which feature in cooking, design, art and fashion. If it's been a while since you engaged with colour wheels, here is a quick refresher:

✦ Primary colours are red, yellow and blue.

✦ Secondary colours are the children of each pair of primary colours: orange, green and purple.

✦ Tertiary colours are made up of one primary colour and one secondary colour: amber, chartreuse, vermilion, magenta, violet and teal.

Primary colour dishes tend to be comprised of a beige food like noodles, pasta or rice topped with riotous foods like stir-fried red and yellow peppers. Blue and red often turn up in sweet dishes, like a berry-filled Summer Pudding. Secondary colour dishes are less shouty. They draw on a large range of orange, green and purple fruits and vegetables, which are the foundation of many healthy slaws and salads. On the sweet side, look no further than a batch of Halloween cupcakes!

Tertiary colours, otherwise called the 'in-between' colours, create more complex and alluring dishes. These colours appeal to many a professional chef, home cook, foodie and Instagrammer for visual impact. In the traditional RYB system, tertiary colours combine a primary colour with one of two adjacent secondary colours. Here are some examples of foods with tertiary pigments:

✦ Amber: yellow-orange courgette flowers and honey

✦ Chartreuse: yellow-green star fruits and gold kiwi fruits

✦ Vermilion: red-orange red snapper (an exotic fish)

✦ Magenta: red-purple cherries, plums, aubergine and Kalamata olives

✦ Violet: blue-purple blueberries and purple kohlrabi

✦ Teal: blue-green is rarely used in food, but popular with bakers when icing cakes

There are different ways to combine colours, based on the following palettes:

✦ An **analogous** colour palette – You pick a colour and pair it with the adjacent colours on the wheel. If the colour was yellow, the adjacent colours would be amber and chartreuse. The effect will be harmonious and easy to look at, like a stuffed yellow pepper with some amber courgettes and chartreuse herbs.

✦ A **complementary** palette – You pick a colour and pair it with the colour that is directly opposite on the wheel. Were you to choose yellow, for example, the complementary colour would be purple. You often see this pairing used in lemon tarts, where the cook has placed a few blackcurrants on top.

✦ A **secondary** palette – Much simpler to work out. The only colours incorporated into a dish would be orange, green and purple.

✦ A **tertiary** palette – More complicated given that there are six colours in contention. My hunch is that you pair up opposite tertiary colours. That means that magenta would pair with chartreuse, and violet would pair with amber.

Another way into Colourful Riots is nature.

Bold-coloured foods turn up in hot, tropical places like India, the Caribbean, Hawaii and South-East Asia. In these countries, there are lots of primary red and yellow foods, and secondary orange and green foods. Depending on how those foods are cooked, it follows that cooks will introduce amber, chartreuse and vermilion foods into their local dishes. You can see these in Hawaiian poke bowls, South Indian curries and Thai pad krapow.

Lush-coloured foods show up in hot, drier countries surrounding the Mediterranean Sea. These run from western Portugal through Turkey to eastern Syria. As they have less rainfall and lower temperatures compared to tropical countries, the range of colours here expands to include some primary blue and secondary purple fruits and vegetables, enveloping tertiary magenta and violet colours. Think Greek salads, Italian pizzas and Turkish freekeh salads. On page 151 you'll see a great example of a vegan bowl made up of purple, orange and green tertiary colours.'

Temperate countries, including swathes of North American states, the United Kingdom, northern European countries and cooler ones in the southern hemisphere (Chile, New Zealand) favour primary red and blue, and secondary green and purple fruits and vegetables. Fresh yellow and orange fruits and vegetables rely on importation. Traditional recipes will nudge you towards tertiary magenta and violet, with some amber coming through via courgettes at the height of summer. We can see these colours in beetroot salads, stuffed courgette flowers and cherry pies.

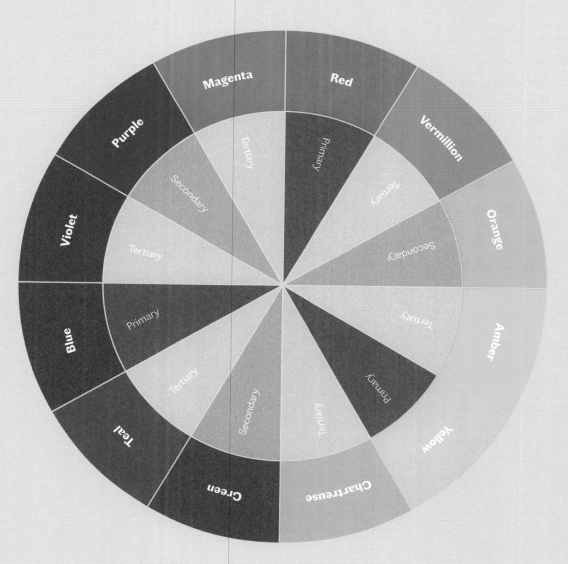

It is easy to identify **Nutritious Colours** in nature because each pigment found in foods has a specific set of health benefits. I am far from an expert in this area of science, but there are plenty of articles on healthy eating and many websites where you can find information. Here are some things I learnt from the British Heart Foundation that might interest you.

✦ **Red** foods contain lycopene, one of the most powerful antioxidants found in nature. Lycopene is active against cardiovascular disease and the aging of cells in the body. Red foods include beetroots, red peppers and chillies, watermelon, tomatoes, pink grapefruit, radishes, cranberries, raspberries and pomegranates (which you could use in a Middle Eastern jewelled couscous salad).

✦ **Yellow** and **orange** foods contain beta-carotene, famous for its ability to protect the skin and promote tanning. It's also a potent anti-tumour agent that strengthens the immune and reproductive systems, preventing cellular aging and protecting eyesight. Yellow-orange foods include butternut squashes, carrots, courgettes, peaches, melons, mangoes, apricots, citrus fruits and sweet potatoes (which you could turn into a curry with spinach and chickpeas).

✦ **Blue** and **purple** foods contain anthocyanins, which are antioxidants and anti-aging flavonoids. They are especially able to strengthen the capillaries and prevent atherosclerosis. Blue-purple foods include blueberries, blackberries, blackcurrants, cherries, figs, purple kohlrabi, dark grapes, plums and aubergines (which you could bake into an aubergine parmigiana).

✦ **Green** foods contain chlorophyll, which is anti-anaemic and cleanses the blood, shapes up the heart and regulates the level of cholesterol in the blood. Green foods include asparagus, avocado, green apples, kiwis, broccoli, brussels sprouts, green cabbage, spinach, chicory, turnip greens, green beans, rocket, nettle, lettuces, kale and peas (which you could use many of in a vegetarian biriyani).

✦ **White** and **beige** foods contain sulphur. The sulphur compounds are antithrombotic, thinning the blood, protecting bone tissue, reducing blood cholesterol and helping fight cancer. White and beige foods include onions, potatoes, cauliflowers, mushrooms, garlic, ginger, bananas, Jerusalem artichokes, leeks and parsnips (which you could turn into a gently spiced soup).

Using colours in cooking requires the same skills as those needed by artists, fashionistas and decorators. Too many colours overwhelm, while too many similar colours disappoint. Broadly, the *main ingredient* in the dish determines the colour scheme.

While you can have oodles of fun creating colourful dishes, it has to be said that the easiest way to make a savoury dish 'pop' is to choose a white, off-white or beige canvas (noodles, pasta, potatoes, rice, toasted bread, etc.), to which you add bold and lush colours with a complementary final flourish. However, you won't want do this all the time and it's not difficult to add colour with herbs, spices (such as turmeric or saffron), condiments, sauces and garnishes, where the main proteins, vegetables, nuts and dairy elements of a dish are less vibrant.

Happily, you can go to town when it comes to colouring sweet dishes. They too may be underpinned by beige by-products (cakes, trifle sponges, ladyfingers, pie crusts), but this is where fresh fruits, candied fruits, sugar-coated petals, jewel-coloured nuts like pistachios and brightly coloured jellies come into their own.

What you *do* need to avoid is introducing colours simply for effect. The one disadvantage of bringing artistry into cooking is the rise of food styling. I think we all know that some recipes get a tart-up at the end of the cooking process. I do it and I don't doubt many of my friends do it too, but my little tricks pale in comparison to pro-food stylists. I am on Instagram, and not a day passes without me seeing at least a dozen beautiful, colourful dishes. This, I am totally fine with.

What I less like about food styling is chucking foods into (or onto) a perfectly good dish that really should not be there. In my view, the most-used food in this respect over the last few years is pomegranate seeds. These have a sweet and sour taste and, as we learnt from those taste pairings we looked at earlier, these jewelled seeds don't go well with salty foods like fish and shellfish, yet I routinely see them sprinkled over these foods. In the end, despite my love of colour and the importance of creating visually appealing dishes, taste and flavour trump appearance every time.

My journey with colours

I was never afraid of using colour in cooking from the get-go, despite a lack of rainbow foods when I first started cooking. Fruit and vegetables were green, purple or blue with a few red ones and the odd yellow (typically lemons). Avocados were in circulation, but few people bought them. Coconuts, figs, limes, mangoes, pineapples and pomegranates were around, but they were pricey. Once I was in Australia, of course, I was just like a child in a sweet shop. Bold and lush-coloured foods became my best friends in the kitchen and I could not get enough of them. Nowadays, those 'sweet shops' are everywhere and our supermarkets teem with colourful food from all four corners of the world.

For all the lucky breaks that I have had, some recipes I choose (or create) inevitably fall short on the colour front. One bright green sauce shown in a cook book I bought came out more grey-green in my saucepan. There were many saffron-scented risottos that looked nothing like the vermillion photoshopped dish staring back at me. It's easy to feel frustrated in those moments where things don't quite go to plan, especially if you've spent a lot of time preparing and cooking, despite the dish being delicious. When that happens to me now, I simply cheat.

My secret weapon in the kitchen is food gels. Good quality food gels are completely safe, thoroughly bland and relatively inexpensive. I reach for them before, or during, cooking when I want to accentuate one or more of the colours in a dish. These days, if I want to make a mayonnaise-based green sauce charged with spinach, chervil, parsley and tarragon, I add a speck of bright green gel. I also add food gels to soups, stocks and desserts. They do have their limitations and you have to go carefully when you add them. I use a cocktail stick, which I dip into the gel, no more than half a fingernail deep to begin with, then swirl into the mixture. Before you wonder what happens if, and indeed when, my prawn cocktail sauce looks more beige than pink, I do get the cocktail stick out, with no guilt at all.

My **Stardust Tip** for using colours in cooking is to start with appetisers, dressings, salads and sauces, and build up your confidence towards using colours in main dishes and desserts. While aromas, textures and tastes are the heart of cooking, to colour or *not* colour is a deal-breaker. Turning out beige food seven days a week will not bring you joy and happiness. Using colours in dishes will also release the artist in you, which will pay dividends when you are serving up your latest creation.

Turn over now for some super colourful dishes.

The more colorful the food, the better... that means vegetables and fruits.

Misty May-Treanor

POKE BOWL

Poke bowls are all the more fabulous for their presentation, but in reality, it's all about the freshness of the foods and the nutritional benefits. The main protein is traditionally fish, usually tuna or salmon. Make sure the fish is very fresh and you can't go wrong!

Preparation time: 30 minutes | Cooking time: 45 minutes | Serves 2

INGREDIENTS

200g sushi rice

25ml rice vinegar

5g salt

15g sugar

200g sashimi-grade salmon fillet

50ml light soy sauce

1 tbsp white caster sugar

1 tsp Japanese furikake seasoning

1 tsp chilli flakes

1 tbsp lime juice

25g cucumber, sliced

25g radishes, sliced

25g carrot, grated

25g red cabbage, shredded

1 avocado, cubed

1 tsp white or black sesame seeds

Chopped fresh coriander, to garnish

METHOD

1. Prepare the fresh vegetables for slicing, shredding and grating.

2. Place the sushi rice in a bowl and cover with cold water. Stir until the water turns a milky white colour, then drain the rice in a colander and return it to the bowl. Repeat this three times, until the water is clear, then leave the rice to soak in fresh water for 15 minutes.

3. Drain the rice and add it to a large saucepan with 250ml of water. Put the lid on, bring to the boil, then turn the heat down to low and let the rice simmer for about 15 to 20 minutes without removing the lid. After this time, take the pan off the heat and leave the rice to steam for a further 10 to 15 minutes, again without removing the lid.

4. While the rice is cooking, make the sushi vinegar. In a small saucepan, combine the rice vinegar, salt and sugar. Heat until the sugar and salt have dissolved, then leave to cool.

5. Drain off any remaining liquid in the steamed rice, then stir through the sushi vinegar. Dice the salmon into 2.5cm cubes, place in a separate bowl, and toss the raw fish in the soy sauce, caster sugar, furikake seasoning, chilli flakes and lime juice.

6. Place the rice in a serving bowl, add the prepared vegetables, avocado and salmon one by one, then garnish with the sesame seeds and fresh coriander.

NOTES

Not everyone loves the seaweed hints in the furikake seasoning, so try a little pinch on a spoonful of sushi rice before using in the recipe. If it is not to your taste, you can omit this.

CHIPOTLE BEAN BURRITOS

The bright colours of the salads and garnishes – tomatoes, avocado, chilli and coriander – really stand out against the dark chipotle beans. Feel free to swap in any ingredients you prefer to make it your own. This recipe is not only healthy and vegan, but spicy, fresh and damn tasty.

Preparation time: 10 minutes | Cooking time: 20 minutes | Serves 2 (makes 4 burritos)

INGREDIENTS

150g wholegrain rice

Salt, to taste

400g tinned black beans

1 tbsp rapeseed oil

1 clove of garlic, crushed

1 tbsp chipotle paste

4 tortilla wraps

1 little gem lettuce, shredded

8 cherry tomatoes, halved

1 avocado, sliced

½ red onion, sliced

½ bunch of coriander, chopped

60g cashew nuts, roughly chopped

½ chilli, deseeded and finely sliced (optional)

1 lime, halved

Salsa of your choice

METHOD

1. Boil the rice for about 15 minutes in seasoned water until cooked through. Drain, rinse and season to taste with salt, then set to one side.

2. Prepare all your raw fillings while the rice is boiling, to make your life easy when it's time to build your burritos.

3. 5 minutes before the rice is ready, drain and rinse the black beans. Heat the rapeseed oil in a frying pan on a medium heat and add the crushed garlic. Fry for no more than a minute, being careful not to burn it. Stir in the chipotle paste and the black beans. If they dry out, just stir in 1 or 2 teaspoons of water.

4. Keep the chipotle beans on a low heat and begin to build your burritos. Lay the tortilla wraps out flat and, starting about a third of the way up, layer up your ingredients. Start with two spoonfuls of rice, then add another couple of the chipotle black beans, followed by some shredded lettuce, a couple of cherry tomato halves and a few slices of avocado and red onion, being careful not to overfill the wraps.

5. Next, sprinkle on some coriander, cashew nuts and chilli (if using). Finish with a squeeze of lime juice and a little dollop of salsa.

6. Fold in one end of the wrap as tightly as possible and then roll up into a neat cylinder. If anything falls out, just drop it back in at the open end. Repeat with the other wraps.

NOTES

Wrap the burritos in tin foil before serving if you are worried about them collapsing, or to pack them up for an on-the-go lunch.

MEZZE SHARING PLATE

Most foods and condiments needed for a mezze are regularly stocked in my kitchen, so I pop out to the shops for a couple of fresh foods, like figs and grapes. The key to keeping the plate interesting is choosing bright colours to lift the tabbouleh, hummus and cream cheese.

Preparation time: 20 minutes | Cooking time: 20 minutes | Serves 2

INGREDIENTS

8 mini sweet peppers

90g light soft cream cheese (I use Philadelphia)

Pitta breads

Green and Kalamata olives

2 pots of hummus (shop-bought is fine)

2 pickled cucumbers, sliced

4 fresh figs, quartered

Handful of red grapes

For the tabbouleh

4 cherry tomatoes, diced

2 spring onions, finely chopped

$\frac{1}{4}$ cucumber, diced

Small bunch of fresh parsley, finely chopped

6-8 fresh mint leaves, finely chopped

2 tbsp lime or lemon juice

2 tbsp extra virgin olive oil

100g medium-ground bulgur wheat

2 tsp olive oil

Pinch of salt

METHOD

1. First, prepare the fresh ingredients for the sharing plate. Cut the tops off the mini peppers and use a teaspoon to push the cream cheese into the cavities. Slice the pitta breads.

2. For the tabbouleh, place the cherry tomatoes, spring onions, cucumber and herbs in a bowl, then stir through the lime juice and extra virgin olive oil.

3. Place the bulgur wheat in a small saucepan with 100ml of water. Add the oil and salt. Bring to a simmer, then cover and cook over a low heat until tender (about 10 minutes). Let the bulgur stand (still covered) for a further 10 minutes. Fluff with a fork and leave to cool.

4. Once cooled, add enough bulgur wheat to the tabbouleh mixture so that it's present but doesn't become the main ingredient. The idea is have a little bulgur with the salad, rather than a salad with the bulgur!

5. Place all the different components for the mezze on a large serving plate along with a big bowl of the tabbouleh. Arrange them in an appealing way and dive in!

NOTES

Don't use fine bulgur wheat for the tabbouleh as the grains are already parboiled.

Whatever you choose to include in your mezze, make sure you have plenty of contrasting colours and tastes on the plate.

AUSSIE SWEETCORN & PEA FRITTERS

Vibrant colours often turn up in breakfasts and brunches and this dish definitely makes the grade. Inspired by Sydney chef Bill Granger, I've upped the spice and introduced a few more colourful foods. I love the textures in this dish too. It's bright, tasty and the perfect way to start a weekend.

Preparation time: 15 minutes | Cooking time: 15-20 minutes | Serves 2

INGREDIENTS

2 corn on the cob

1 beef tomato

50g red onion, diced

125g plain flour

1 tsp baking powder

$\frac{1}{4}$ tsp salt

$\frac{1}{4}$ tsp cayenne

1 tbsp white caster sugar

2 large eggs

125ml whole milk

50g peas

50g red pepper, diced

30g fresh coriander, chopped

4 rashers of dry-cured streaky bacon (I like The Jolly Hog brand)

4 tbsp rapeseed or safflower oil

30g baby spinach or rocket

METHOD

1. Preheat the oven to 70°c. Cut the sweetcorn kernels off the cobs using a sharp knife and place them in a large bowl. Slice the beef tomato horizontally to get thick rounds, put them on a plate and season lightly with salt. Put the diced onion into a bowl of cold water and leave to soften for 10 minutes.

2. Sift the flour, baking powder, salt and cayenne into a large bowl. Stir in the sugar and make a well in the centre. In a smaller bowl, whisk together the eggs and milk. Add the egg mixture to the dry ingredients and stir to create a batter. Switch to a whisk once all the ingredients are incorporated to make the mixture smoother.

3. Drain the red onion and pat dry with kitchen towel, then add it to the bowl of sweetcorn kernels along with the peas, red pepper and coriander. Stir in just enough batter to bind everything together (you won't need to use all the batter).

4. Heat up your grill and cook the bacon rashers until crispy. Meanwhile, add 2 tablespoons of the oil to a large non-stick frying pan on a medium-high heat. Drop 120ml of the sweetcorn mixture into the pan and quickly shape it into a round, then repeat to make 2 fritters.

5. Keep an eye on the fritters as they cook. Each needs 2 minutes on the first side, or until golden. Flip the fritters in the order you added them and cook for another 2 minutes.

6. Using a slotted metal spatula, transfer the first batch of fritters to a baking tray and pop them in the oven to keep warm. Make 2 more fritters with the remaining mixture and oil.

7. Assemble the dish. Place a fritter on each plate and top with a slice of beef tomato, some baby spinach or rocket and a bacon rasher. Stack another fritter on top and repeat with the tomato, spinach and bacon, then serve.

NOTES

It's better to use fresh corn rather than tinned, as the pre-cooked kernels would be too soft in the batter.

TOFFEE BLACKBERRY PAVLOVA

This is a lovely autumnal dessert starring the unusual but excellent combination of blackberry and toffee. Adding colourful foods to desserts based on meringue is key to make them look appealing. The contrasting colours here are very striking; pillowy white meringue, deep purple berries and bright green pistachios always impress.

Preparation time: 25 minutes | Cooking time: 1 hour 45 minutes | Serves 4

INGREDIENTS

2 tsp cornflour

2 tsp vanilla extract

2 tsp apple cider vinegar

5 large egg whites

300g golden caster sugar

50g nibbed green pistachio slivers (I use the Sous Chef brand)

500g fresh blackberries

3 tsp Chambord liqueur (optional)

400ml double cream

3 tbsp toffee sauce (I use Márdel dulce de leche)

METHOD

1. Preheat the oven to 120°c and line a baking tray (with a minimum width of 28cm) with non-stick baking paper.

2. Blend the cornflour, vanilla and vinegar to a smooth paste in a small bowl. In a separate bowl, whisk the egg whites until stiff. Gradually whisk the sugar into the whites to make a thick and glossy meringue mixture, then add the cornflour paste with a splash of water and whisk until combined.

3. With a large serving spoon, spread the meringue mixture onto the lined baking tray to form a circle about 24cm in diameter, without flattening it.

4. Swirl the edges of the meringue with the back of the spoon to create soft folds and peaks. Scatter half of the nibbed pistachios over the meringue and place in the preheated oven to bake for 1 hour.

5. After baking, tap the meringue on any side to test for crispness. Turn off the oven and leave the meringue to cool with the oven door ajar for about 45 minutes.

6. Meanwhile, prepare the blackberries. You may want to wear gloves here as the juice can stain. Place them in a colander and dip into a bowl of cold water to rinse gently. Drain the blackberries, then put them into a glass or china dish. Using your fingers, gently coat the blackberries with the Chambord (if using) and leave them to marinate.

7. Lightly whip the cream until soft and billowy. Add the toffee sauce to the cream and very gently stir it in with a fork (don't use the whisk for this).

8. Remove the meringue from the oven and make sure it has cooled completely. Drop a large spoonful of the toffee cream onto the meringue and spread carefully, working from the outer ring into the centre and leaving 3 to 4cm of the outside edge of the meringue bare. Do not worry if the meringue cracks here and there, it happens!

9. Dot the marinated berries over the cream, again working from the outside in. Scatter the remaining nibbed pistachios over the whole pavlova and serve immediately.

DIVAS

During many creative endeavours – writing, composing, painting – there comes the moment when the artist adds the final detail to complete their work. It could be the radical change in direction of a story's plot, the 'button' at the end of a song, or the flying goat in a Marc Chagall painting. Garnishes are the final details in the world of cooking and the stock-in-trade of every professional chef, as well as many keen home cooks.

Garnishes are made of edible components like vegetables, fruits, herbs, spices and sauces. Cooks choose these for visual impact or to add further layers of flavour. Michelin-starred chefs use them perfectly for both. What makes the difference between a good garnish and a bad one is creativity and thought. Good garnishes exhibit unforgettable flair. Bad ones result in ugly, complete flops.

'Garnering a dish' is a phrase that fell out of favour somewhere in the 1970s 'Me' decade. Swathes of tomato roses, carrot flowers and pineapple hedgehogs turned up on tacky buffet tables at every social bash. Just looking at them made you want to turn back and walk away. Once foodies declared war on these lurid toppings, in came a new generation of chefs who reworked garnishes and replaced the word garner with words like adorn, decorate, embellish and gild.

I do love garnering a dish, but just hearing the other g-word gives me the heebie-jeebies. Memories of my early attempts at making devilled eggs (otherwise known as stuffed eggs) left me cold, as did the one time I made one of those tacky tomato roses. The way I got around this was to give garnishes a new name: divas. Just like real-life divas, they bring out the bling, create an impression, are sometimes overconfident and always interesting. Whether you go with the traditional name, use mine, or make up one of your own, divas are a must-have in your magical kitchen.

Getting to grips with Divas

✦ Diva Food

✦ Diva Combos

✦ Diva Cheat Sheets

When you tear some flat-leaf parsley over scrambled egg or a cheesy risotto, you are adding a **Diva Food**. Parsley is a classic one. It is simple and creates some visual appeal. If you cut some leafy green vegetables like lettuce, spinach or Swiss chard into long, thin strips (known as chiffonade) and throw them over a bowl of clear broth or soup, that, too, is a Diva Food. But it is also a small step up from the first, introducing more flavours.

Both Diva Foods are authentic, but the time it takes to make them and the degree of original creativity is very different. And while the best of them are mostly about flavour and visual impact, they can help you (and those you're cooking for) identify the underlying foods of a dish too, such as using cumin to bring out the carrot, sweet potato and butternut squash in a soup.

Relatively everyday ingredients that you can deploy include:

✦ Edible flowers – borage, elderflower, nasturtiums and pansies

✦ Fruits – berries, cape gooseberries, kumquats, lemons and limes, oranges and pomegranates (the larger the fruit, the more options for its use, such as zesting, slicing and cutting into wedges)

✦ Green herbs – basil, bay leaves, chervil, chives, coriander, microgreens, oregano and thyme

✦ Nuts – almonds, hazelnuts, peanuts, pecans, pistachios and walnuts (often toasted for better flavour and crunch)

✦ Salad greens – chicory, endive, lettuces, rocket and spring onions (the latter finely chopped)

✦ Seeds – chia, nigella, poppy, pumpkin, sesame, sunflower (the smaller the seed, the less impact it will have)

✦ Spices – cinnamon bark and star anise

✦ Vegetables – carrots, radishes and tomatoes

✦ Wafers – crackers, Melba toasts and ice-cream cones

I divide my Diva Foods into three categories: fresh, dried and confectioned. The fresh ones go into my fridge. Dried ones go into my pantry. Confectioned ones are stored in my baking cupboard, which I have to confess is massively over-stocked (physician, heal thyself!). As with scents and condiments, you do not need to stock shedloads of ingredients. Just make sure you have a small stock of colourful and textured ones that will perk up most of your dishes.

Diva Combos are more interesting, often intricate and mostly original. When you bring together a mix of foods – a few herbs, an edible flower, some chopped nuts and toasted seeds – and add them to a dish such as fillet of sea bass with a lemon garlic sauce, that is a good combo. When it came to remaking garnishes in the 80s, the first chefs out of the blocks were French and American. They were followed by another generation of chefs in the 90s and 00s who were into the very cool art (and science) of molecular gastronomy.

What paved the way for a reassessment of garnishes was the need to reflect new approaches to cooking. The French were ditching some of the heavier sauces for which they were famous, and pivoting towards lighter, more delicate dishes and eye-catching presentation. Across the pond, American chefs on the West Coast were also heavily into presentation. Rather than lighten up their dishes, they began combining flavours from different countries and regions, and introduced rather more bold and colourful Diva Combos. Phrases like Californian Cuisine, Pacific Flavours and Cal-Asian emerged and inspired chefs in like-minded countries with similar temperatures, like Australia.

Diva Combos went up another notch a decade later, when chefs like Heston Blumenthal, Grant Achatz and Ferran Adrià started mucking around with various natural gums and hydrocolloids, which paved the way for even more spectacular Diva Combos. If you've heard about Fusion Cuisine (American), Nouvelle Cuisine (French), Mod Oz (Australian) and Modernist Cuisine (Global), you can see where and how those dire 70s garnishes morphed into the perfectly plated world of food styling in which we live now.

The one thing you do have to remember about Diva Combos is that contrast is everything, and this applies to colour, shape and texture. Here are some key points to remember:

✦ Creamy, silky, velvety and pulpy dishes (soups, mousses) call for crunchy and crispy divas and combos need to have contrasting colours, such as sourdough croutons, seeds and roasted anything (like pancetta) scattered over a tomato soup.

✦ Starchy and slightly sticky dishes like pastas, noodles and rice with a sauce also need crunchy and crispy divas. Colour contrasts work best when the colour of the diva is the opposite of the protein or vegetable ingredient, such as strips of sundried red peppers over broccoli or chopped purple basil over lemon.

✦ Dishes that contain chewy foods cooked with moist heat (meat and fish curries) call for something light and crisp, like white coconut flakes and edible flowers sprinkled over a rich auburn Indonesian curry. Those same foods cooked with dry heat (roasts, grills and bakes) call for light gremolata and other thinner condiments like pesto and chimichurri.

✦ Sweet and savoury salads can be dressed with a wide range of foods in contrasting textures and colours, including seeds and herbs.

You have to be brutal with yourself when it comes to choosing Diva Foods.

There is no use buying bunches of fresh herbs, exotic fruits and shedloads of confectionery if you don't need them. I have a couple of **Diva Cheat Sheets** that I work from, largely to make sure I don't forget to make the most of my Diva Foods and sink into a routine where I focus on a few usual suspects. I also update my sheets as new products come onto the market. Persian Fairy Floss was one I added a couple of years ago, and other products that I buy from the amazing G. Detou deli in Paris. I never come out of that place without finding something new and funky that is promptly added to my collection.

Before international travel really took off in the 90s, most home cooks relied on TV chefs and cook books to help us see what types of divas were trending. Nowadays, we get to travel all over the world, photographing and sharing pictures of dishes from Nordic delis to Cape Malay mashups, with Diva Foods revealed in magnificent technicolour. While there are endless examples of simple, interesting and mouth-watering ones on the internet, I find cookery magazines the best source for understanding them. The quality ones do a good job of telling me which ingredients make up the diva, how to make it and what equipment I need to have on hand. You won't need these for everyday cooking, but if you want to up your presentation skills, at least a few pieces of kit might need to be procured.

The Diva Cheat Sheets overleaf list the Diva Foods I routinely stock in my kitchen and from these I can bring together striking Diva Combos for savoury and sweet dishes. The cheat sheets do not cover every potential food that could be a contender. When I'm trying out a new cuisine I focus on getting a few dishes right before I play around with the toppings. For me, substance has to come before style. However, it does mean my choices are very much western-oriented. Next time round, I hope I can make my cheat sheets more inclusive.

Shortcuts
Savoury Diva Foods

Colourful

Chives
A favourite with any white food, like potatoes, eggs, sour cream.

Edible Flowers
Blue cornflowers, yellow marigolds, rose petals, nasturtiums.

Dried Fruit
Accentuate a hearty casserole, stew or tagine with dried fruits.

Gremolata
Chopped lemon zest, garlic, parsley and anchovy (used in ossobuco).

Chimichurri, Persillade, Pesto
All condiments that double up as a garnish.

Microgreens
Red amaranth, purple basil, red vein sorrel, red chard.

Most green herbs

Textural

Amandine
Toasted almonds, often added to boiled or steamed green vegetables.

Nuts
All able to double up as a garnish, fresh or heated.

Seeds
Also able to double up as a garnish, though tiny seeds may get lost in a crowd.

Croutons
Toasted bread, great for soups, particularly with French onion soup.

Toasts
Fried onions, more suitable to red meats (and steak in particular).

Parmesan Crisps
Oven-cooked, resembling biscuits.

Chorizo, Lardons and Prosciutto
Oven-cooked, good with pastas and white fish

Star Anise
Just for the look of it!

Shortcuts
Sweet Diva Foods

Colourful

Cocoa Powder
For dusting over nuts or something creamy like tiramisu.

Edible Flowers
Sugar-coated rose petals and other delicate flowers.

Edible Leaves
Gold or silver, and simply beautiful. Not to be wasted!

Exotic Fruits
Cape gooseberries, star fruit, golden kiwifruit.

Fruit Peels and Shavings
Fresh or candied, mostly jewel-coloured.

Herbs
Sweet and aromatic mint and basil.

Powders
Strawberry, raspberry and beetroot for dusting silky desserts.

Textural

Amaretti Biscuits
Hard on the outside, chewy in the middle.
Good for crumbling over desserts.

Chocolate & Praline Crisps
Small round biscuits.

Cinder Toffee
Also known as puff candy or sea foam. Shows up in Crunchie bars.

Chocolate and Mint 'Matchsticks'
Good for decorating cakes.

Coconut (Shredded or Flaked)
Great for exotic fruits and rum-based desserts.

Meringues
Basis of pavlova. Great crumbled in Eton mess.

Nuts
Able to double up as a garnish, fresh or heated (latter recommended).

Persian Fairy Floss
Not candy floss, but utterly divine. Comes in spring colours.

Pink Pralines
French confectionery, not to be confused with Italian pink sugared almonds.

Seeds
Able to double up as a garnish. More forgiving for delicate and silky desserts.

Sprinkles
Fun and crackly, though perhaps best kept back for children's parties.

Wafers
Best paired with ice creams, but can double up with sorbets at a pinch.

My journey with divas

I think I have always liked decorating my dishes, but getting beyond the steak-and-cherry-tomatoes era took me some time. When the French, American and Modern Cuisine lot were reworking the concept of garnishes, I bought tons of cookery books and magazines on finishes, as some chefs refer to them. I would pore over them, looking for the latest inventions to road-test in my kitchen.

It's safe to say that most of my efforts fell short due to a lack of skill and, while I was nothing but determined to improve, in the end I lowered my expectations. Having said that, my trials did give me a better understanding of the importance of contrasting colours and textures. While I love my Diva Foods, in the end there is no desperate need to create them every time you cook. To misquote Shakespeare, do not fall into thinking "a cherry, a cherry, my sundae for a cherry!"

My **Stardust Tip** for working with finishes is not to see them as an option, but rather a step in the cooking process. As was the case for colours, introducing both nutritional benefits and visual impact is the best way to go. Fresh and dried Diva Foods are not expensive, and even a few edible flowers from your local florist or garden will brighten up your dishes. Do keep your dried and confectioned ones in a cool place and check the use-by dates routinely. Some of these are quite pricy, so keep an eye on your budget. Nonetheless, you – and those you're cooking for – will always appreciate those final details.

Next up are recipes to showcase those lovely toppings for prettying up your dishes.

Know how to garnish food so that it is more appealing to the eye
and even more flavorful than before.

Marilyn Vos Savant

INDIAN SHARING PLATE

I like sharing plates and mostly make these when I have friends over for a relaxed supper. Why not push the boat out from time to time on a special occasion: new job, new flat, or just to show someone your appreciation? Here are a few easy ideas, which are great served as they are or with accompaniments such as mango chutney. This recipe is for 2 people, so double or triple the ingredients for a larger group.

Preparation time: 35 minutes, plus 30 minutes marinating | Cooking time: 30 minutes | Serves 2

INGREDIENTS

Prawn Poppadoms

1 small tub of raita

6 ready-to-eat mini poppadoms (I use the Sharwoods brand)

6 cooked and peeled extra-large tiger prawns

Fresh coriander, finely chopped

Pinch of sumac

Saag Paneer Fritters

1 medium egg

50g each milk and self-raising flour

60ml vegetable oil

2 tsp each garam masala and ground turmeric

1 clove of garlic, grated

100g paneer, diced into 1cm cubes

125g baby spinach

3 spring onions, finely sliced

Tandoori Chicken Skewers

2 tbsp natural yoghurt

2 tsp garam masala

1 tsp each ground turmeric and chicken seasoning (optional)

1 large chicken breast, sliced into 3 pieces lengthways then into thin strips

METHOD

Prawn Poppadoms

1. Dollop about a teaspoon of raita onto each mini poppadom, then top with a prawn. Sprinkle on some fresh coriander and a light dusting of sumac. Serve and enjoy!

Saag Paneer Fritters

1. Beat the egg and milk together in a bowl, whisk in the flour to make a thick batter, then season with salt and pepper to taste. Cover and set aside.

2. In another bowl, whisk half the oil with the spices and garlic. Add the paneer and mix gently until the cheese is coated. Put a wok on a medium-high heat, then add the spiced paneer and cook for about 5 minutes, or until it starts to colour.

3. Add the spinach and spring onions, cook until the spinach has wilted, then pour the contents of the wok into a sieve over a bowl. Discard any leftover oil and leave the paneer mixture in the sieve to cool for 5 minutes at room temperature.

4. In a clean pan, heat the remaining clean oil until it starts to shimmer. Meanwhile, beat the rested batter with a fork to loosen it, then gently fold in the cooled paneer mixture.

5. Put 2 heaped tablespoons of the mixture into the hot oil for each fritter. Do not crowd the pan or the fritters won't crisp up. Cook the fritters until golden, which should take 2 to 3 minutes on each side, then place in a low oven on a wire rack to keep warm.

Tandoori Chicken Skewers

1. Thoroughly mix the yoghurt with the spices and seasoning in a bowl. Fold the chicken strips into the yoghurt marinade, cover and place in the fridge to rest for at least 30 minutes. I like to leave it for a few hours.

2. Meanwhile, soak some mini wooden skewers in water to ensure they don't burn during cooking. When the chicken is ready, preheat the grill to medium high.

3. Thread 3 pieces of marinated chicken onto each skewer and grill for 15 minutes, turning halfway through. A little charring only adds to the flavour! Serve hot.

SEA BASS WITH TURMERIC & COCONUT SAUCE

I love the Caribbean for the sun and the flavours of its cuisine. Fish is abundant there and often plated on a colourful sauce alongside a fresh, green salad. Back at home, I like a mildly spicy fish dish with a creamy tropical sauce, garnished with a few savoury Diva Foods.

Preparation time: 15 minutes | Cooking time: 15 minutes | Serves 2

INGREDIENTS

60g red cabbage, sliced

30g carrot, grated

30g baby spinach, torn

Salt and pepper

2 tbsp olive oil

2 sea bass fillets

1 red chilli, finely chopped

Small handful of edible flowers (pansies, violas, borage)

30g toasted coconut flakes (I buy these from health food stores)

For the sauce

1 tbsp coconut oil

$\frac{1}{2}$ brown onion, chopped

2cm fresh root ginger, peeled and minced

150ml vegetable stock

1 tbsp ground turmeric

$\frac{1}{4}$ tsp sea salt

175ml coconut milk

$\frac{1}{2}$ lemon, juiced

METHOD

1. For the sauce, melt the coconut oil in a small saucepan on a medium heat. Add the onion and sweat for 5 minutes, or until lightly browned and translucent. Add the ginger and cook while stirring until fragrant.

2. Add the stock, turmeric and sea salt to the pan and mix to combine everything. Bring to the boil, then cover and turn down to a simmer to cook on a low heat for 5 minutes.

3. Leave the flavoured stock to cool for 5 minutes before transferring it to a blender (I do this in my NutriBullet). Add the coconut milk and lemon juice, then blend until fully smooth and combined. Taste the sauce to check the saltiness and add another quarter teaspoon if needed. Keep at room temperature.

4. Combine the red cabbage, carrot and baby spinach in a small bowl. Add a tablespoon of very cold water, season with salt and pepper, give the vegetables a shake and set aside. This keeps them fresh while you cook the fish.

5. Lightly coat the base of a non-stick frying pan with olive oil then place the pan over a medium-high heat.

6. Once the pan is hot, season the sea bass fillets with salt and pepper and lay them into the pan skin-side down. Press the fillets with a fish slice to prevent curling and ensure the skin cooks evenly.

7. Cook the fish for 3 to 4 minutes until the skin is nicely golden and crisp, then carefully turn the fillets over to cook for 1 minute on the other side, until the flesh is opaque.

8. To serve, pour the turmeric and coconut sauce onto the plates. Place the fish in the centre, sprinkle over some red chilli, then arrange the vegetables and flowers on one side. Finally, scatter the toasted coconut flakes over the sauce on the other side.

NOTES

For a special dish like this, I tend to buy the fillets from a fishmonger, fresh on the day. While the coconut milk gives this dish its flavours, you could swap it out for soya milk if preferred.

AROMATIC BURRATA BRUNCH

Burrata is an Italian cheese made from buffalo mozzarella and cream that flows out when sliced open. It's expensive but a real delight. However, it needs some showy Diva Foods to make the whole dish sparkle. I've chosen to add fragrant Asian notes that align with the lovely nutty aroma of sesame oil.

Preparation time: 10 minutes | Cooking time: 5 minutes | Serves 2

INGREDIENTS

1 tsp chopped hazelnuts

2 fresh burrata

2 slices of fresh sourdough bread, lightly toasted

Handful of rocket

1 tsp Thai basil leaves

1 tsp sea salt

For the dressing

30ml sesame oil

30ml rapeseed or safflower oil

1 tsp coriander seeds

1 tsp red chilli flakes

METHOD

1. For the dressing, pour the oils into a small jug and stir to combine. Crush the coriander seeds to a coarse powder with a mortar and pestle, then add this to the jug with the chilli flakes and stir again.

2. Transfer the dressing to a small saucepan over a medium heat and bring the temperature to 120°c. Cook for a couple of minutes. Leave to cool at room temperature while you prepare the rest of the dish.

3. Toast the chopped hazelnuts in a dry shallow pan for 2 to 3 minutes, or until you can smell the nutty aromas.

4. Place the burrata on serving plates and drizzle over the cooled dressing. Add the toasted sourdough and rocket to the plates.

5. From a height, sprinkle the toasted hazelnuts, Thai basil leaves and sea salt over the dressed burrata. Serve immediately.

NOTES

Because the dressing is heated, you need to use oils that have a higher smoke point, so don't substitute the rapeseed or safflower oil with olive oil.

If you want to make this a more substantial dish, you can add some roasted butternut squash slices or wedges to the plates, served warm rather than straight out of the oven.

FRUIT HULLABALOO

The exotic flavours in this beautiful dessert make it so much more than a fruit salad. I like to use 5 or 6 fruits with similar properties and have mostly used watery fruits here, for consistency. You can experiment with different fruits, but bear in mind that some might not work as well with the flavours in the jelly and syrup. Fantastic on a hot summer's day and a great example of a Diva dish.

Preparation time: 20 minutes, plus 3 hours setting | Cooking time: 5 minutes | Serves 2

INGREDIENTS

½ honeydew melon

1 dragon fruit (approx. 250g)

150g strawberries

75g blueberries

10 fresh cherries

Small handful of pomegranate seeds, to garnish

1 tsp rose sugar (I use the Sous Chef brand)

For the jelly

2 titanium-strength gelatine leaves (or 3 ordinary strength)

60ml pear and elderflower cordial

½ tsp Poire Williams (Williams pear liqueur)

For the cream

100ml double cream

1 tsp vanilla bean paste

25g icing sugar

For the syrup

25g caster sugar

1 tsp rose blossom syrup (I use the Monin brand)

1cm fresh root ginger, grated

METHOD

1. Line a 20cm square tin or dish with cling film, pushing it right into the corners.

2. For the jelly, soften the gelatine in cold water for 4 to 5 minutes. Drain and squeeze out the excess water. Heat the cordial and liqueur with 200ml of water in a saucepan. Bring to the boil, then remove from the heat. Stir in the gelatine until dissolved. Pour the liquid jelly into a prepared square or rectangular tray (china or glass ideally) and refrigerate for at least 3 hours, or until set.

3. For the cream, whip the ingredients together until soft peaks form. Transfer the mixture into a small, colourful serving bowl. Cover and refrigerate until needed.

4. For the syrup, put the ingredients into a saucepan with 60ml of water and cook over a medium heat for 5 to 6 minutes, until the sugar has dissolved and the volume of liquid has reduced to a syrupy consistency. Cool and strain the syrup through a fine sieve, discarding the ginger solids. Set aside at room temperature.

5. Prepare the fruit. Use a double melon baller to create small and medium balls of honeydew (you should get about 10 of each). Top and tail the dragon fruit, then halve it lengthways. I like to peel one half and leave the skin on the other for colour. Cut both halves into 1-2cm cubes. Slice two thirds of the strawberries vertically and halve the rest. Leave some cherries whole and halve the rest. Toss all the fruits in the cooled syrup and leave to stand for no more than 5 minutes , otherwise the fruit will go soggy.

6. Place the bowl of whipped vanilla cream on a sharing plate (I like to use an oval one). Cut the jelly into 2cm cubes and arrange on the plate with all the fruit. Scatter the pomegranate seeds over the plate.

7. Dust the fruit plate with rose sugar to finish and serve with a small jug of the syrup.

NOTES

Fruit salads are best served at room temperature. If you are making this on a hot day, keep the prepared fruit in a cool place, but not the fridge. Bananas, pears and apples tend to turn brown quickly once cut, so won't look as good on the plate.

OCCASIONS

In mid-2021, when I came to edit this final chapter, I read it and paused.

What I had hoped to share with you was how to plan, prepare and produce a multi-course meal for a special occasion. Up to this point in the book, the focus had been on the basic elements: choosing the foods you like to eat, pairing foods for taste and flavour, adding foodstuffs for depth of flavour, taking your dishes up a notch through layering, embedding nutritious foods using colours and eye-catching toppings for visual impact. Cooking for occasions was the last step in this learning process; the crowning moment, where all the other steps would come together based on your personal journey with cooking.

I'd hoped that you would be feeling confident enough to create a meal like this for your soulmate, bestie, friends and family – coming up with your own 'carte du jour' (menu) for such an occasion – all while enjoying yourself rather than stressing out.

Life changes though. Well before the pandemic hit, entertaining by hosting a formal dinner party had already fallen by the wayside: too Gordon Gekko, too glitzy, too rigid. In its place, people went for easy-going cooking. Potlucks and sharing plates took off, marking the value of friendship and social bonding. Brunches and barbecues stayed the course, but they remained seasonal of course: best in the summer, a little chilly in the winter.

My plan was to share some meal options for any special occasion on which you could build.

When I came to edit this chapter after fifteen months of lockdowns and restrictions, however, I wondered what the future would look like. Would the get-togethers and do's we used to take for granted – weekend brunches, barbecues, afternoon teas, chilli nights and festive days – look different from now on? Whether to scrap what I had written originally and start over, or stick with the original draft and pretend nothing had changed, was a question worth thinking on.

As someone who lived through the last dying days of formal dinners, I'm all for less stress and more time with guests. In the end, I chose not to scrap everything I had written before, while recognising the times certainly are a-changing. On that note, then, let's finish up with some options and tips for creating different occasions to suit a wide variety of guests and gatherings.

Getting to grips with occasions

✦ Occasion Basics

✦ Occasion Options

✦ Occasion Tips

The secret to **Occasion Basics** is creating an agreeable meal, where each course fits together to form a whole, based on a common thread. This is not always the easiest thing to do when you are just starting out. It's like learning to drive, where you start on empty country roads before you take on the more challenging highways and motorways.

The one niggle with cook books that I have read over the years has been a strange reluctance of the writer (chef, cook, foodie) to suggest a few **menus** for the reader, based on the recipes they had included in their book. The same goes for food magazines that give over whole pages to pictures of awesome dishes, beautifully photographed, with the ingredients, tastes and flavours summarised in a brief caption. Rarely, however, do they take the extra step of suggesting other recipes that might come first or follow these dishes. Contrast this with menus for brunches, barbecues and such on the internet and in weekend newspaper supplements, where there are loads of suggestions for a feel-good do.

There is even less attention paid to how you might create a menu for two, three or even four course meals. Not only do I remain convinced that cooking for special occasions is a wonderful thing to do when you want to express your affection for your loved ones, I also suspect that a lot of people are afraid to make a meal like this, simply because they're not sure how to do it 'right'. While I have no intention of bringing back those showy formal dinners, which were largely about status and money, I am keen to strike a balance.

You might assume it is easier to create a meal for 2 people than it is to cook for 6 or 8, or even 20+. In reality, despite all the jobs you have to complete for a special occasion (shopping, prepping and cooking), the hardest job is coming up with the menu. While you might be able to delegate some of those jobs to friends and family ahead of, or on, the day, the menu is basically on you (sorry!).

Your job is to design and create a culinary arc from the first nibble (crostini, blini) to the final morsel (something bite-size and sweet, like an After Eight). In the past, there were principles for getting that arc right, such as stimulating guests' appetites at the beginning of a meal (hence the name 'amuse-bouche' for this course). Other principles included serving a palate cleanser (sorbets, fresh fruit) halfway through the meal, and that having a pastry starter (the infamous vol-au-vents) with a pastry dessert was a firm no-no, as was starting with a creamy soup if the veggies in the main dish were also creamed. While some of these principles are worth knowing, you really do not need to bone up on this stuff.

It's far more important to wrap your head around the different types of occasions that you might want to master, and how to flex the different courses and dishes appropriately. In my experience, there are three basic meal types:

✦ **One-plus** – date nights, romantic dinners, visits from besties or favourite brothers/sisters/cousins and mad aunts and uncles who buy you stuff (just because they can)

✦ **Ten and under** – best for friends, friends of friends, gym-buddies, or a mix of family and friends, where the numbers allow for a degree of intimacy

✦ **Double figures** – anything up to 20+ people, typically served outdoors (such as brunches and barbecues) where the occasion is more of a party

There are **Occasion Options** for different meal types which invites different challenges and ways of approaching them. For example, when it is just you and one other person, you want to spend quality time with them. You do not want to be pan-frying steaks or making pancakes that need flipping every couple of minutes. The challenge here is to choose dishes that you can prep earlier in the day or, better still, the day before. Challenges for larger occasions are more about the logistics and making sure that you show up at your own party: more host, less caterer!

For one-plus occasions, you can make two or three courses as you wish. The best advice I received for this type of meal was to stick with just one cuisine. By doing this, you will be using similar foods, foodstuffs and cooking methods, which makes it easier and quicker for you to cook and chat. If you want to make three courses, you can expand to another cuisine, but choose one in the same neighbourhood. A Scandi-inspired salmon starter that has a mild, fresh marine-y flavour will *not* go well with a meaty, earthy, spicy Moroccan tagine, while a shellfish Portuguese paella based on a traditional sofrito of onion, garlic and tomato *will* go with the coconutty Brazilian egg custard pudding called quindim.

Choose what you want to cook for the main course first. Once you have this pinned down, choose a dish for the starter or dessert course next. If you are up for three courses, pick the starter second, and the dessert third. Remember, there needs to be a common thread based on cuisines, tastes or flavours.

Start with something light, lukewarm or cold, and not too spicy or fruity. Spices might create indigestion, while sugar will dull the appetite. Follow on with a warm or hot main, where at least one of the flavours in that course appeared in the starter, and where there are different textures. If you want to add a dessert, pick out one of the flavours in the main (for example spicy, citrusy or nutty notes) and make sure the textures contrast. So that you can get a feel for this type of meal, here is a menu suggestion for a romantic or intimate occasion, which I have selected from the recipes in this book, where the common thread is southern Mediterranean foods:

✦ Warm salad starter – Spanish Serrano Ham, Spinach & Avocado Salad (page 46)

✦ Hot main – Suzy's Chicken Maryland Supreme (page 48)

✦ Cold topping over hot dessert – Roasted Peaches with Amaretti & Mascarpone (page 96)

For ten and under occasions, there still needs to be a thread running through the dishes and courses. However, with more people, you will probably need to make provisions for different preferences (vegetarian, vegan, keto, gluten-free, halal, et cetera). There are also the logistics of shopping, storing and freezing, prepping ahead, rummaging around for bowls and platters and, especially, getting the timings right for serving. Two tricks here: first, do as much prep as you can before your guests arrive and second, let your guests serve themselves, for which you'll need some big platters and large bowls. Based on my experience, I find it easiest to choose two key tastes (complementary or balanced) and pick dishes in various cuisines that align with those tastes.

Here's a menu suggestion for a weekend lunch or Friday night supper gathering, again based on recipes in this book, with a common thread of sweet and sour tastes:

✦ Cold starter – Tuna Ceviche (page 26)

✦ Hot street food – Chipotle Bean Burritos (page 152)

✦ Warm main – Spiced Ham with Peach Couscous (page 94)

✦ Cold dessert – Fruit Hullabaloo (page 176)

For larger bashes, you have the same challenges as a small gathering, times two. On the other hand, these occasions generally take place outdoors. They also tend to go on for longer. In my experience, despite the logistics, I find these occasions easier compared to smaller gatherings. Most people are happy to have a drink and chat while you stagger the courses over a longer period of time. In these settings, where there has to be something for everyone, I go with a thematic thread. Here are some ideas to inspire you:

✦ **Sizzling and searing** – where the barbecue/pizza oven/rotisserie is the centre of attention. There are lots of salty tastes and crispy textures, which cry out for citrusy and spicy notes and soft, fresh and creamy textures. Early courses need to be generous, as the main courses will take some time to cook. Mushy, velvety and creamy dips from the Levant are a good option, served with wraps, flatbreads and chopped garden salads. Juicy tomatoes, peppers and red onions can accompany cooked fishes, meats and pizza. Once the sizzling is over, bring out some pre-made chilled, silky, creamy desserts. My Bourbon-Glazed Chicken Drumsticks and Seared Steak with Broad Beans could work here (see pages 134 and 70) followed by the Norwegian Cream Pudding (page 30) all scaled up according to the number of guests.

✦ **Cool and classy** – where diverse grazing and sharing platters are abundant. The focus is on raw, fresh and healthy foods, piled up on plates and interspersed with cured meats and fishes. Platters include fruits, cheeses, vegetables and shellfish. Trappings include breads, crackers and focaccias. Chutneys are great for veggies, while spicy Asian sauces go super well with seafood. While there are a number of dishes, the fare is relatively light, so finish with substantial snacks and desserts like gluten-free granola bars; banana, chocolate and lemon loaves; and carrot or courgette cakes with ricotta or mascarpone icings for a sugar hit and extra energy. My Mezze and Indian Sharing Plates (see pages 154 and 170) and Nikkei Sea Bass (page 114) could work here, along with Persian Baklava (page 116).

✦ **Autumnal and smoky** – where the oven does all the hard work by roasting, cooking and baking. The focus is on earthy, smoky, spicy fare. The first dishes out should be heavier and hearty but remember not to make them too spicy. Roasts, whole fishes and weighty root vegetables (like aubergines, butternut squashes and pumpkins) hold up very well to hot spices and salsas. Vegetarian pilau, risottos, fluffy quinoa, fruity couscous, herby tabbouleh and warm bean salads pair perfectly (and aren't too stodgy or filling). To finish, choose a late-summer or autumn berry or stone fruit, baked in (or on top of) a crisp shell, like a frangipane pie or a pillowy meringue. My Saffron & Chilli Prawn Risotto (see page 132) and Rack of Lamb with Spicy Mint Salsa (page 92) could work here, as would the Toffee Blackberry Pavlova (page 158) though again, you might have to double or triple the quantities.

The more people you are cooking for, the more things you will have to consider, so here are a few **Occasion Tips**.

The most exciting moment for me is coming up with a new dream menu. The most anxious moment is in those last few minutes before serving, trying to compose myself and adopt a carefree pose (which I always fail to do, even with my best friends). Do you remember me saying that no two cooks have identical likes and dislikes when it comes to food, which means no two kitchens would stock the same ingredients? Well, I think the same applies to special occasions. Some people rattle off the menu and stick to it, while others weigh up the options and only make a decision at the last minute. Some fret that they have forgotten something, while others just go with the flow. I have read many a book and blog about how to plan and prepare for a special occasion and I've come across some great tips, but in reality, different people plan and prepare differently. So I'm not going to bore you with a long list of things to do. Instead, here are just five tips that have helped me over the years:

Seasonality – most people don't want to eat fresh foods that are totally out of season, despite them being available year-round in supermarkets. Take pineapples and mangoes, for example. Fresh slices at the end of a meal always go down well on a hot day, but not in the depths of winter. If you want to buck the trend, however, I suggest you grill or roast them and pair with a sumptuous dark chocolate sauce or a sweet and sticky coconut rice pudding. This 'rule' does not apply to out-of-season fresh fruits and vegetables for savoury dishes (where they are going to be cooked), like a sweet and sour Hong Kong style dish with chicken and pineapple, or a spicy Sri Lankan mango curry.

Stocktaking – when you have got your dream menu sorted, go through all your cupboards to see how many of the foodstuffs that you need to create it are already there. If you have less than half of the foodstuffs required for your occasion, I suggest you tweak your menu... otherwise, you might be eating baked beans for a week! This might mean a few substitutes (go back to Food Families for a refresher) or possibly a rethink. Despite my love of desserts, if the bank account is looking a bit low, I sacrifice that course first.

Shopping – whether you love shopping or hate it, the last thing you want is a missing ingredient. Neither you, nor anyone around you, wants to run out to the corner shop at the last minute. It is tempting to make one huge shopping list of all the ingredients that you will need, but I find it easier to make two lists. I have one for the foodstuffs (which I buy a few days, or even a week, before) and another for all the fresh foods (which I buy on the day if I can, but no more than the day before). I also pre-order foods that may be in short supply. If I am throwing a large bash, I also clear out one of my pantry shelves and place all the foodstuffs that I will need to use there. I do the same with the fridge, clearing out a space for all the fresh foods. I guarantee that this will make the prep and cooking experience go more smoothly.

Prepping – there's preparation, and then there's pre-preparation. Rarely can you prep everything ahead. Some fruits and vegetables (apples, avocadoes, lettuce, potatoes) turn brown once they are cut and exposed to the air. Fruits that don't brown, like berries, can be prepared a few hours ahead (though if you're incorporating them into creams, wet cheeses and yoghurt, don't add the fruits until serving. Ditto with salad dressings: pre-prep, but don't add them to garden salads until you're ready to plate. Breadcrumbed and deep fried dishes (like my Breadcrumbed Goat's Cheese on page 108) are best served immediately, because the coating will become soggy in the fridge. You do need to make savoury nibbles and dishes for brunches and grazing plates in real time, which makes the cooking experience more intensive. On a more positive note, you can pre-prep most soups and dips up to 24 hours ahead. You can do the same for bean salads, salsas and marinades, but leave out the fresh herbs, as they will spoil, and add them before serving. You can also pre-prep many desserts, like caramels, panna cottas, meringues, muffins, loaves and cakes.

Timings – treat special occasions as you would a festive meal. Make a rough estimate of the time it will take to prepare your foods (to include time for marinating, if relevant). Then jot down the suggesting cooking times for each of the elements in the meal from start to finish, for example fifteen minutes to pan-fry fish, a couple of hours for baked potatoes, three hours for a casserole. Include timings for boiling water to make a stock, cook rice or blanch vegetables. My best tip is to write down a *provisional* time to serve the substantial course, and work around that. Because you know how long the various dishes will take to cook, you will have a feel for when you have to slip out, whether to check something in the oven, or put a saucepan on the heat. It will also help you visualise the hills (where you can do a few quick things in parallel, for example, bringing water to the boil for pasta while you peel, core and quarter pears for the last course, dessert) and troughs (where you can take a break and enjoy yourself). This is the best way to make your occasion work just as you envisaged it!

My journey with occasions

Luckily for me, my early years of working in professional kitchens gave me quite a few insights into cooking a multi-course meal. Everything revolves around the menu. Produce is 'king' and every food has to be fresh, fresh, fresh. Seasonal foods that come and go give the chefs a chance to do something different and creative. Not to mention the aesthetics; as I have said before, people *do* eat with their eyes.

In those restaurants, I learnt about standardised recipes: the number of servings, portion size, exact quantities of each ingredient, specific directions, cooking temperatures and times, plating and the (dreaded) garnishing. I also learnt how to nudge guests away from dishes that the chef would not recommend pairing together, largely because the guests tended to blame the restaurant for making their own bad choices!

My first boyfriend in Sydney was a hotel manager. Fringe benefits included free accommodation in the hotel for him and me both. Most evenings, when my day job was over, I would join him and his chef for a drink when they were discussing menus for the next day. I never pursued formal qualifications, but I am a 'cooking native' – someone who chose to build on what I had learnt in my early years. I kept learning, I made mistakes, but ultimately, I became a decent cook. Hardly a MasterChef contender, but able to master the basics with a few tricks up my sleeve to boot.

It's no secret that I wrote this book after coming across all sorts of articles on the divide between those who cook at home and those who buy takeaways and eat out. All the signs suggested the divide was generation-related. Compared to my generation, when the school curriculum included home economics, cooking was a skill that you could acquire relatively easily. Nowadays, maybe not so easily. And, so, I chose to write this book for those who love to eat, are happy to cook and follow a recipe, but say they aren't *that* confident in the kitchen. In the writing of it, I realised that I consider myself a cooking native and a digital immigrant, while you might be a digital native and a cooking immigrant. How's that for symmetry!

So, we are at the end now, and I hope you have got something out of this book and been inspired to start creating your own magical kitchen. Remember: food first, dishes second. Remember, too, the nine steps:

- ✦ **Foundations** first – foods, tastes, flavours
- ✦ **Fixtures** second – scents, condiments, potions
- ✦ **Finishes** third – colours, divas, occasions

Now that you have gone through all these steps, feel free to go back to those you're most interested in and want to learn more about. The culinary world is always evolving and there are plenty of cuisines to try, fall in love with or dismiss. I wish you all the best.

Cooking for people is an enormously significant expression of generosity and soulfulness, and entertaining is a way to be both generous and creative. You're sharing your life with people. Of course, it's also an expression of your own need for approval and applause. Nothing wrong with that.

Ted Allen

Recipe Index

Glossary

Appetiser – a small dish of food or a drink before a meal (or the main course of a meal) to stimulate one's appetite.

Cuisine – a style or method of cooking, characteristic of a particular country, region or establishment, as in "a cuisine based on local ingredients" or "this restaurant is famous for its spicy cuisine."

Dish – food prepared in a particular way, as in "a dish of sautéed potatoes" or "fresh fish dishes."

Entrée – a dish served between the first and main courses at a formal dinner.

Intermezzo – something small, light and refreshing that helps cleanse the palate between courses. Typically, though not exclusively, a sorbet.

Main – the centrepiece of a multi-course meal, as in "the main dish was poached salmon."

Recipe – a set of instructions for preparing a dish.

Digest

Helpful References

Samin Nosrat – Salt, Fat, Acid, Heat

Sybil Kapoor – Sight, Smell, Touch, Taste, Sound

Sophie Grigson – Spices

James Briscione, Brooke Parkhurst – The Flavor Matrix

Niki Segnit – The Flavour Thesaurus, Lateral Cooking

Lior Lev Sercarz – The Spice Companion

Christine Ingram – The World Encyclopaedia of Cooking Ingredients

Nik Sharma – The Flavor Equation

Delores Custer – Food Styling

Helpful Reads

Diane Henry – A Bird in the Hand

Tom Kerridge – Best Ever Dishes, Outdoor Cooking

Bill Granger – Bill's Food, Simply Bill

Simon Hopkinson – Simon Hopkinson Cooks, Roast Chicken and Other Stories

Nigella Lawson – How To Eat, Feast, How To Be A Domestic Goddess

Rick Stein – Fish & Shellfish, The Road to Mexico

Donna Hay – Flavours, The Instant Cook

Oliver Rowe – Food for All Seasons

Annie Bell – Gorgeous Cakes

Hisako Ogita – I Love Macarons

Jamie Oliver – Jamie Cooks Italy

Nigel Slater – The Kitchen Diaries, The Kitchen Diaries II

Martha Stewart – Martha Stewart's Vegetables

Michael Roux – Sauces: Sweet and Savoury, Classic and New

Peter Gordon – Savour: Salads for all Seasons

Mark Bittman – Dinner for Everyone

Vivian Lui – Eat California

Jeanine Donofrio – The Love & Lemons Cookbook

Alice Waters – Chez Panisse Menu Cookbook

Nargisse Benkabbou – Casablanca

Kate Marshall is the face of **@yourmagicalkitchen** on Instagram. She is a self-taught cook and an unabashed foodie. Her working life has straddled radio, television, publishing and government in the UK and Australia. Kate's passion is helping people who love to eat, like to cook and can follow a recipe, but want to be more confident in their own kitchen. Her Instagram is chock-a-block with cuisines from every corner of the world, where she connects the dots for aspiring cooks who want to expand their culinary horizons, all in a non-scientific way. Her first published book takes readers on a personalised journey through nine easy steps to help them become a creative force in their kitchen, based on the foods they love to eat. Embedded in these steps are Kate's personal and humorous stories, explaining how she learnt to cook and the mistakes and lessons she encountered on the way.